한 권으로 끝내는 초등 영문법

Grammar!

 Happy House

조이 쌤(Inyoung Joy Hwang) 소개

어렸을 때부터 영어를 좋아했고, 통역사의 꿈을 키웠던 조이 쌤은 한동대 국제어문학부에서 영어를 전공하고, 숙명여자대학교에서 국제영어교사 테솔 과정을 수료했습니다. 대학교 재학 시절부터 많은 아이들에게 영어를 지도했으며, 어학전문 출판사에서 편집자로 근무하며 한국 어린이들의 환경에 맞는 영어 교재를 기획, 개발하였습니다. 영어와 교육을 더욱 전문적으로 공부하기 위해 미국 텍사스로 유학을 떠나 기독교교육학 석사학위를 취득하고, 미국의 한 사립학교에서 인턴교사로 일했으며, 계속해서 영어 교재를 집필하고 있습니다. 교육에는 사람을 바꿀만한 힘이 있다고 믿고, 학교를 세우는 꿈을 꾸고 있습니다.

안녕, 친구들. **한 권으로 끝내는 초등 영문법**의 저자 조이 쌤이에요.
여러분을 만나게 되어 진심으로 반가워요.

여러분은 영어를 무엇이라고 생각하나요?
선생님은 여러분에게 **"영어는 언어다!"**라고 말하고 싶어요.
우리가 한국에서 한국말로 의사소통을 하는 것처럼,
영어는 의사소통을 위해 세계적으로 쓰이는 언어예요.

영문법을 공부하는 이유는 단지 학교에서 좋은 시험 성적을 받기 위해서가 아니에요.
영문법을 공부하는 이유는 '**영어로 의사소통을 잘하기 위해서**'입니다.

영어는 미국, 영국, 캐나다, 호주, 뉴질랜드에서 모국어로 쓰이고, 그 외에도 아일랜드 공화국,
싱가포르, 말레이시아, 필리핀, 자메이카, 네덜란드, 스웨덴, 덴마크, 이스라엘 등의
많은 나라에서 공용어처럼 사용하고 있으며, 제2외국어로 영어를 사용하는 나라 또한 많아요.
75억의 세계 인구 중, 20%인 15억 인구가 영어를 사용하고 있지요.
(세계에는 7,000여 개의 언어가 있다는 사실!)
영어라는 언어에 재미를 붙여 잘 배우면,
여러분이 꿈꾸고 실현해나갈 수 있는 일은 무궁무진하게 많아진답니다.

영문법을 배우면 우리가 하고자 하는 말을 더 구체적으로 명확하게 전달할 수 있고,
상대가 전하는 메시지도 더 쉽게 이해할 수 있어요.
한 권으로 끝내는 초등 영문법은 여러분이 알아야 할 영문법을
쉽고, 꼼꼼하게 익힐 수 있도록 만들어진 책이에요.
우리 친구들이 영문법을 잘 배워서 영어로 말하고, 듣고, 읽고, 쓰는 것을
즐겁게 할 수 있도록 조이 쌤이 도와줄게요.

여러분 모두를 응원하며,
미국 텍사스에서 조이 쌤

책의 구성과 특징

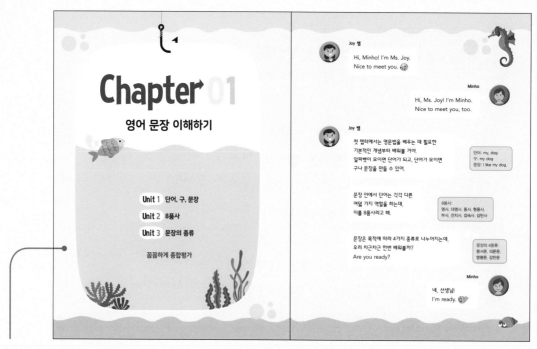

본격적인 학습에 앞서 각 챕터에서 배울 문법 개념을 미리 살펴봅니다.
선생님과 학생의 대화 형식으로 문법 내용에 쉽고 흥미롭게 접근할 수 있도록 도와줍니다.

문법 설명 문법 개념을 간략한 설명과 표, 실용적인 예문들로 이해하기 쉽게 설명합니다.

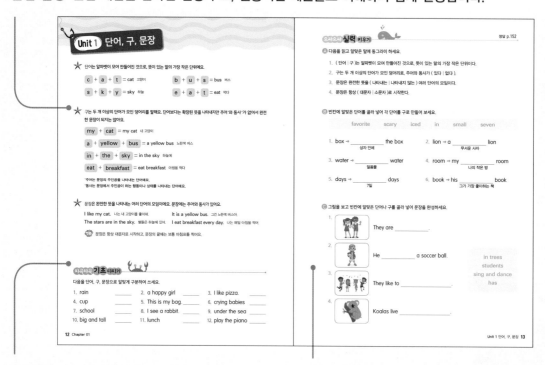

차곡차곡 기초 다지기 학습한 문법을 잘 이해했는지 기초적인 문제를 풀며 확인합니다.

으쌰으쌰 실력 키우기 다양한 응용 문제들을 풀며 문법 개념을 탄탄히 익힐 수 있습니다.

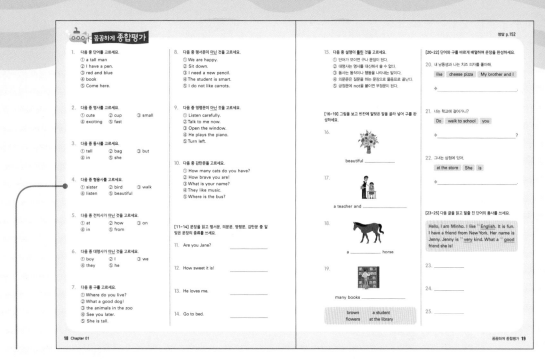

꼼꼼하게 종합평가 각 챕터에서 배운 내용을 최종적으로 점검하는 문제들로 구성했습니다.
내신에 자주 출제되는 객관식 문제와 서술형 문제를 실전처럼 풀어볼 수 있습니다.

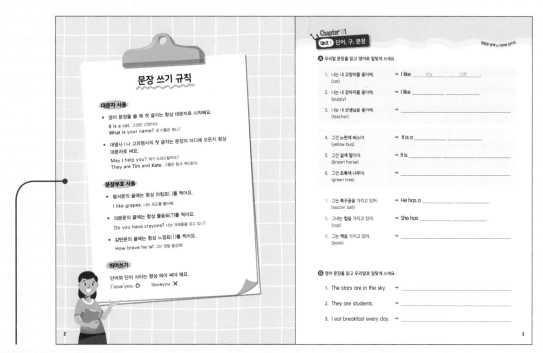

문장 쓰기 노트 각 유닛에서 배운 문법을 적용한 문장을 써보는 연습을 할 수 있습니다.
문장 쓰기 연습을 통해 영문법을 마스터하고 영작 실력을 쌓을 수 있습니다.

홈페이지 다운로드 자료 www.ihappyhouse.co.kr

- 정답
- 각 유닛에 나온 필수 단어를 정리한 단어 리스트
- 영어로, 또 우리말로 써보며 외우는 단어 테스트
- 문법 학습에 도움을 주는 예문 번역

목차

영문법 용어 풀이

구
두 개 이상의 단어가 모인 것을 말한다.
ex) my cat, a yellow bus

주어
문장의 주인공을 일컫는 말로, 보통 주어로 문장을 시작한다.

목적어
문장에서 주어가 하는 행동의 대상을 나타내며 동사 뒤에 위치한다.

보어
주어나 목적어를 보충하여 설명하는 말이다.

8품사
말의 8가지 종류인 명사, 대명사, 동사, 형용사, 부사, 전치사, 접속사, 감탄사를 의미하며, 품사는 각각의 고유한 역할이 있다.

명사
사람이나 사물, 장소, 개념 등의 이름을 나타낸다.

대명사
명사를 대신해서 쓰이며 인칭대명사(I, you, he, she, it, we, they)와 지시대명사(this, that, these, those)가 있다.

동사
문장에서 주어가 하는 동작이나 행동을 나타내며 be동사, 일반동사, 조동사가 있다.

형용사
명사를 꾸며주며, 모양이나 상태를 나타낸다.

부사
형용사, 동사, 다른 부사를 꾸며준다.

전치사
명사 앞에 놓여서 시간, 위치, 방향 등을 나타낸다.

접속사
단어나 구, 문장을 연결한다.

감탄사
강한 느낌이나 놀란 감정을 표현한다.

be동사
동사이지만 주어의 움직임을 나타내지 않고 주어와 다른 단어들을 연결한다. 주어의 인칭과 수, 시제에 따라 am, are, is로 모양이 달라진다.

일반동사
문장에서 주어의 움직임을 나타낸다. 주어가 3인칭 단수이고 현재 시제일 때는 동사의 끝에 -(e)s를 붙이고, 과거를 나타낼 때는 -(e)d를 붙인다.

조동사
동사를 도와 그 의미를 보태는 역할을 하며 can, may, must, should 등이 있다.

평서문
생각이나 정보, 감정을 평범하게 진술하는 문장이다.

긍정문
평서문에서 부정의 뜻이 없는 문장이다.

부정문
평서문에서 부정의 뜻인 not이 들어간 문장이다.

의문문
무엇인가를 묻는 문장으로 문장 끝에 물음표를 쓴다.

인칭
주어가 자신이면 1인칭, 상대방이면 2인칭, 그 외에는 3인칭이다. 1인칭의 복수형은 우리, 2인칭의 복수형은 너희들, 3인칭의 복수형은 그들이다.

단수
명사의 수가 하나인 것을 말한다.

복수
명사의 수가 두 개 이상인 것을 말한다.

관사
명사 앞에 붙는 말로 부정관사 a/an과 정관사 the가 있다. 부정관사 a/an은 막연한 '하나'를 뜻하고, 정관사 the는 '그'라는 뜻으로 특정한 명사를 가리킨다.

빈도부사
문장에서 주어가 하는 일의 횟수를 알려주는 부사이다.

동명사
동사를 명사로 품사를 바꾼 것으로, 동사원형에 -ing를 붙여 만든다.

to부정사
동사 앞에 to를 붙여 명사, 형용사, 부사 등 여러 가지 품사로 바꾸어 쓰는 것을 말한다.

의문사
문장 맨 앞에 와서 의문문을 만들며 who, when, where, what, how, why 등이 있다.

Chapter 01

영어 문장 이해하기

Joy 쌤

Hi, Minho! I'm Ms. Joy.
Nice to meet you.

Minho

Hi, Ms. Joy! I'm Minho.
Nice to meet you, too.

Joy 쌤

첫 챕터에서는 영문법을 배우는 데 필요한
기본적인 개념부터 배워볼 거야.
알파벳이 모이면 단어가 되고, 단어가 모이면
구나 문장을 만들 수 있어.

> 단어: my, dog
> 구: my dog
> 문장: I like my dog.

문장 안에서 단어는 각각 다른
여덟 가지 역할을 하는데,
이를 8품사라고 해.

> 8품사:
> 명사, 대명사, 동사, 형용사,
> 부사, 전치사, 접속사, 감탄사

문장은 목적에 따라 4가지 종류로 나누어지는데,
우리 차근차근 한번 배워볼까?
Are you ready?

> 문장의 4종류:
> 평서문, 의문문,
> 명령문, 감탄문

Minho

네, 선생님!
I'm ready.

Unit 1 단어, 구, 문장

 단어는 알파벳이 모여 만들어진 것으로, 뜻이 있는 말의 가장 작은 단위예요.

c + a + t = cat 고양이   b + u + s = bus 버스

s + k + y = sky 하늘   e + a + t = eat 먹다

 구는 두 개 이상의 단어가 모인 덩어리를 말해요. 단어보다는 확장된 뜻을 나타내지만 주어*와 동사*가 없어서 완전한 문장이 되지는 않아요.

my + cat = my cat 내 고양이

a + yellow + bus = a yellow bus 노란색 버스

in + the + sky = in the sky 하늘에

eat + breakfast = eat breakfast 아침을 먹다

*주어는 문장의 주인공을 나타내는 단어예요.
*동사는 문장에서 주인공이 하는 행동이나 상태를 나타내는 단어예요.

 문장은 완전한 뜻을 나타내는 여러 단어의 모임이에요. 문장에는 주어와 동사가 있어요.

I like my cat. 나는 내 고양이를 좋아해.   It is a yellow bus. 그건 노란색 버스야.

The stars are in the sky. 별들은 하늘에 있어.   I eat breakfast every day. 나는 매일 아침을 먹어.

Tip 문장은 항상 대문자로 시작하고, 문장의 끝에는 보통 마침표를 찍어요.

 차곡차곡 **기초** 다지기

다음을 단어, 구, 문장으로 알맞게 구분하여 쓰세요.

1. rain _____   2. a happy girl _____   3. I like pizza. _____

4. cup _____   5. This is my bag. _____   6. crying babies _____

7. school _____   8. I see a rabbit. _____   9. under the sea _____

10. big and tall _____   11. lunch _____   12. play the piano _____

으쌰으쌰 실력 키우기

A 다음을 읽고 알맞은 말에 동그라미 하세요.

1. (단어 | 구)는 알파벳이 모여 만들어진 것으로, 뜻이 있는 말의 가장 작은 단위이다.

2. 구는 두 개 이상의 단어가 모인 덩어리로, 주어와 동사가 (있다 | 없다).

3. 문장은 완전한 뜻을 (나타내는 | 나타내지 않는) 여러 단어의 모임이다.

4. 문장은 항상 (대문자 | 소문자)로 시작한다.

B 빈칸에 알맞은 단어를 골라 넣어 각 단어를 구로 만들어 보세요.

favorite   scary   iced   in   small   seven

1. box → _____ the box
   상자 안에

2. lion → a _____ lion
   무서운 사자

3. water → _____ water
   얼음물

4. room → my _____ room
   나의 작은 방

5. days → _____ days
   7일

6. book → his _____ book
   그가 가장 좋아하는 책

C 그림을 보고 빈칸에 알맞은 단어나 구를 골라 넣어 문장을 완성하세요.

1. They are _____.

2.  He _____ a soccer ball.

3.  They like to _____.

4.  Koalas live _____.

in trees
students
sing and dance
has

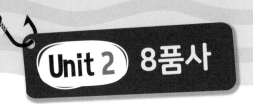

Unit 2 8품사

⭐ 영어의 단어는 문장 속에서 각각의 고유한 역할을 해요. 단어를 역할에 따라 나눈 갈래를 품사라고 해요. 영어의 품사는 여덟 개가 있어요.

1. 명사는 사람, 사물, 장소 등의 이름을 나타내는 단어예요.

boy 소년　　Minho 민호　　book 책　　dog 개　　school 학교　　Korea 한국

2. 대명사는 명사를 대신하여 사용하는 단어예요.

my dad ➡ he 그　　a bag ➡ it 그것　　Jenny and Tim ➡ they 그들

3. 동사는 문장의 주어가 하는 동작이나 행동을 나타내는 단어예요.

run 달리다　　eat 먹다　　play 놀다　　teach 가르치다　　love 사랑하다

4. 형용사는 명사를 꾸며주는 단어로, 모양이나 상태, 수량 등을 나타내요.

<u>red</u> roses 빨간 장미　　a <u>happy</u> girl 행복한 소녀　　<u>three</u> cookies 세 개의 쿠키

5. 부사는 형용사나 동사, 다른 부사를 꾸며주는 단어예요.

Flowers are <u>very</u> beautiful. 꽃은 매우 아름다워.　　She runs <u>fast</u>. 그녀는 빨리 달려.

6. 전치사는 명사 앞에 놓여서 문장 안에서 다른 단어들과의 관계를 나타내는 단어예요.

The cat is <u>in</u> the box. 고양이가 상자 <u>안에</u> 있어.　　I get up <u>at</u> 6 o'clock. 나는 여섯 시에 일어나.

7. 접속사는 단어나 구, 문장을 연결하는 역할을 하는 단어예요.

a rabbit <u>and</u> a turtle 토끼와 거북이　　I want milk <u>or</u> juice. 나는 우유나 주스를 원해.

8. 감탄사는 강한 느낌이나 놀란 감정을 표현할 때 사용하는 단어예요.

wow 우와　　oh 오　　ouch 아야　　oops 이런, 아이고

차곡차곡 **기초** 다지기

다음 단어의 품사가 무엇인지 쓰세요.

1. he _____

2. Seoul _____

3. small _____

4. in _____

5. at _____

6. very _____

7. ice cream _____

8. student _____

9. wow _____

10. and _____

11. read _____

12. or _____

A 다음 문장에서 괄호 안의 품사를 찾아 동그라미 하세요.

1. I love baseball and basketball. (접속사)
2. The dog is very cute. (부사)
3. Frogs jump high. (동사)
4. She is tall. (대명사)
5. Tom is a smart cat. (형용사)
6. The gift is on the table. (전치사)
7. Ouch! It hurts! (감탄사)
8. It is a desk. (명사)

B 괄호 안의 품사에 해당하는 단어를 빈칸에 골라 넣어 문장을 완성하세요.

in   writes   friend   so   hot   wow

1. A good book is a good _____. (명사)
2. The milk is very _____. (형용사)
3. My family lives _____ London. (전치사)
4. _____! I'm happy for you. (감탄사)
5. You are _____ wonderful. (부사)
6. Paul _____ a letter. (동사)

C 다음 문장에서 밑줄 친 단어의 품사를 차례대로 쓰세요.

1. Horses <u>run</u> <u>fast</u>. → _____ _____
2. <u>We</u> sleep <u>at</u> <u>night</u>. → _____ _____ _____
3. Mary <u>has</u> <u>two</u> sons <u>and</u> one daughter. → _____ _____ _____
4. <u>Oh</u>, look at the <u>big</u> <u>bear</u>! → _____ _____ _____

Unit 3 문장의 종류

⭐ 문장은 말하는 목적에 따라 평서문, 의문문, 명령문, 감탄문으로 나누어져요.

1. 평서문은 생각이나 정보를 평범하게 진술하는 문장으로 항상 마침표로 끝나요. 평서문은 대개 〈주어 + 동사〉 순이고, 부정어인 not을 사용하여 부정문을 만들 수 있어요.

| 긍정문 | We are hungry. 우리는 배가 고파. | 부정문 | We are not hungry. 우리는 배가 고프지 않아. |

| 긍정문 | I like winter. 나는 겨울이 좋아. | 부정문 | I do not like winter. 나는 겨울을 좋아하지 않아. |

2. 의문문은 무엇인가를 묻는 문장으로 문장 끝에 물음표를 찍어요.

Are you okay? 너 괜찮니?

Do you like ice cream? 너는 아이스크림을 좋아하니?

When is your birthday? 너의 생일은 언제니?

3. 명령문은 상대방에게 무엇을 하도록 시키는 문장으로 보통 동사로 시작해요. 명령문의 맨 앞이나 맨 뒤에 please를 붙이면 정중하게 요청하는 표현이 됩니다.

Come here. 이리 와.　　　　　　　　Open your book. 책을 펴라.

Please be quiet. 조용히 해주세요.　　Close the door, please. 문을 닫아주세요.

4. 감탄문은 느낌이나 감정을 강하게 표현하는 문장으로 문장 끝에 느낌표를 찍어요.

What a beautiful day it is! 정말 아름다운 날씨다!

How brave she is! 그녀는 정말 용감해!

차곡차곡 **기초** 다지기

다음 설명에 알맞은 문장의 종류를 연결하세요.

1. 무엇인가를 묻는 문장　　　　　　　•　　　　　　　　　　　• 평서문

2. 생각이나 정보를 진술하는 문장　　•　　　　　　　　　　　• 명령문

3. 느낌이나 감정을 강하게 표현하는 문장 •　　　　　　　　　• 의문문

4. 상대방에게 무엇을 하도록 시키는 문장 •　　　　　　　　　• 감탄문

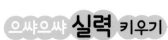
Ⓐ 문장을 읽고 알맞은 문장의 종류를 쓰세요.

1. My favorite color is blue.   → _____

2. What a cute dog it is!   → _____

3. Are you late?   → _____

4. Give me some water.   → _____

Ⓑ 대화에 알맞은 문장을 골라 쓰세요.

1. A: What is your name?

   B: _____

2. A: I lost my cat.

   B: _____

3. A: It is cold. _____

   B: OK.

4. A: _____

   B: Yes, I do.

Do you like bananas?
My name is Jade.
Close the door.
How sad it is!

Ⓒ 괄호 안의 문장의 종류에 맞게 빈칸에 알맞은 단어를 골라 넣어 문장을 완성하세요.

what   is   how   stand

1. _____ is this? (의문문)

2. _____ nice you are! (감탄문)

3. This _____ my ball. (평서문)

4. _____ up. (명령문)

1. 다음 중 단어를 고르세요.

① a tall man
② I have a pen.
③ red and blue
④ book
⑤ Come here.

2. 다음 중 명사를 고르세요.

① cute   ② cup   ③ small
④ exciting   ⑤ fast

3. 다음 중 동사를 고르세요.

① tell   ② bag   ③ but
④ in   ⑤ she

4. 다음 중 형용사를 고르세요.

① sister   ② bird   ③ walk
④ listen   ⑤ beautiful

5. 다음 중 전치사가 아닌 것을 고르세요.

① at   ② how   ③ on
④ in   ⑤ from

6. 다음 중 대명사가 아닌 것을 고르세요.

① boy   ② I   ③ we
④ they   ⑤ he

7. 다음 중 구를 고르세요.

① Where do you live?
② What a good dog!
③ the animals in the zoo
④ See you later.
⑤ She is tall.

8. 다음 중 평서문이 아닌 것을 고르세요.

① We are happy.
② Sit down.
③ I need a new pencil.
④ The student is smart.
⑤ I do not like carrots.

9. 다음 중 명령문이 아닌 것을 고르세요.

① Listen carefully.
② Talk to me now.
③ Open the window.
④ He plays the piano.
⑤ Turn left.

10. 다음 중 감탄문을 고르세요.

① How many cats do you have?
② How brave you are!
③ What is your name?
④ They like music.
⑤ Where is the bus?

[11~14] 문장을 읽고 평서문, 의문문, 명령문, 감탄문 중 알맞은 문장의 종류를 쓰세요.

11. Are you Jane?   _____

12. How sweet it is!   _____

13. He loves me.   _____

14. Go to bed.   _____

15. 다음 중 설명이 <u>틀린</u> 것을 고르세요.

① 단어가 모이면 구나 문장이 된다.
② 대명사는 명사를 대신해서 쓸 수 없다.
③ 동사는 동작이나 행동을 나타내는 말이다.
④ 의문문은 질문을 하는 문장으로 물음표로 끝난다.
⑤ 긍정문에 **not**을 붙이면 부정문이 된다.

[16~19] 그림을 보고 빈칸에 알맞은 말을 골라 넣어 구를 완성하세요.

16.

beautiful _____

17.

a teacher and _____

18.

a _____ horse

19.

many books _____

brown	a student
flowers	at the library

[20~22] 단어와 구를 바르게 배열하여 문장을 완성하세요.

20. 내 남동생과 나는 치즈 피자를 좋아해.

like   cheese pizza   My brother and I

➡ _____ .

21. 너는 학교에 걸어가니?

Do   walk to school   you

➡ _____ ?

22. 그녀는 상점에 있어.

at the store   She   is

➡ _____ .

[23~25] 다음 글을 읽고 밑줄 친 단어의 품사를 쓰세요.

Hello, I am Minho. I like [23]<u>English</u>. It is fun. I have a friend from New York. Her name is Jenny. Jenny is [24]<u>very</u> kind. What a [25]<u>good</u> friend she is!

23. _____

24. _____

25. _____

Chapter 02

명사와 관사

꼼꼼하게 종합평가

Joy 쌤

이번 챕터에서는 명사와 관사에 대해 배울
거야. 지난번에 8품사 배운 거 기억나니?

Minho

영어의 8품사는 명사, 대명사, 동사,
형용사, 부사, 전치사, 접속사, 감탄사예요.

Joy 쌤

Great!
품사는 각각의 고유한 역할이 있지. 명사의 역할이 뭐였지?

Minho

명사는 사람, 사물, 장소 등의 이름을 나타내는 역할을 해요.
선생님, 그런데 관사는 뭐예요?

Joy 쌤

관사는 명사에 씌우는 모자 같은 역할을 하는 단어야.
명사 앞에 붙는 a, an, the 같은 단어가 바로 관사야.
명사 앞에 붙어서 명사의 수나 특징을 알려주지.

명사와 관사를 자세히 설명해줄게.
Let's get started!

Unit 1 셀 수 있는 명사

⭐ 명사는 사람, 사물, 장소, 개념 등의 이름을 나타내는 말이에요.

| 사람 | boy, doctor, Jane | 사물 | book, apple, desk |
| 장소 | house, park, Seoul | 개념 | love, time, music |

⭐ 명사는 셀 수 있는 명사와 셀 수 없는 명사로 나눌 수 있어요. 셀 수 있는 명사는 수에 따라 단수와 복수로 나뉘어요.

1. **단수**는 명사의 수가 하나인 것을 말하며, 명사 앞에 a나 an을 붙여요.

   a book   a car   a teacher   an apple   an elephant   an umbrella

2. **복수**는 명사의 수가 두 개 이상인 것을 말해요. 명사 뒤에 보통 -s를 붙여 복수형을 만드는데, 다음과 같은 몇 가지 규칙이 있어요.

대부분의 명사	+ -s	book ➡ books, teacher ➡ teachers, cookie ➡ cookies, boy ➡ boys
s, x, ch, sh, '자음 + o'로 끝나는 명사	+ -es	glass ➡ glasses, box ➡ boxes, watch ➡ watches, dish ➡ dishes, potato ➡ potatoes
'자음 + y'로 끝나는 명사	y ➡ i + -es	puppy ➡ puppies, baby ➡ babies
f, fe로 끝나는 명사	f, fe ➡ v + -es	leaf ➡ leaves, knife ➡ knives, wolf ➡ wolves
단수와 복수가 같은 명사		fish ➡ fish, deer ➡ deer, sheep ➡ sheep
불규칙적으로 변하는 명사		man ➡ men, woman ➡ women, foot ➡ feet, tooth ➡ teeth, goose ➡ geese, mouse ➡ mice, child ➡ children

 차곡차곡 **기초** 다지기

다음 그림에서 찾을 수 있는 명사에 모두 동그라미 하세요.

book	clock	go	happy
chair	eat	like	desk
good	student	big	teacher

으쌰으쌰 **실력** 키우기

Ⓐ 다음 명사의 복수형에 동그라미 하세요.

1. bus ➡ buses   buss

2. bench ➡ benchs   benches

3. man ➡ mans   men

4. potato ➡ potatoes   potatos

5. leaf ➡ leafs   leaves

6. chair ➡ chairs   chaires

7. tooth ➡ tooths   teeth

8. baby ➡ babies   babys

Ⓑ 다음 명사의 복수형을 쓰세요.

1. a car ➡ two _____

2. a fish ➡ two _____

3. a fox ➡ two _____

4. a pencil ➡ two _____

5. a lady ➡ two _____

6. a mouse ➡ two _____

7. a knife ➡ two _____

8. a dish ➡ two _____

Ⓒ 밑줄 친 부분을 바르게 고쳐 쓰세요.

1. I have two <u>dog</u>.   ➡ _____

2. I like <u>strawberrys</u>.   ➡ _____

3. I need two <u>tomatos</u>.   ➡ _____

4. She has three <u>childs</u>.   ➡ _____

5. I see two <u>boxs</u>.   ➡ _____

6. My <u>foots</u> are small.   ➡ _____

Unit 2 셀 수 없는 명사

★ '사과', '책'처럼 개수를 셀 수 있는 명사와 달리 세상에 단 하나밖에 없거나 눈에 보이지 않아서 셀 수 없는 명사도 있어요. 셀 수 없는 명사의 종류에는 고유명사, 추상명사, 물질명사가 있어요.

1. 고유명사는 세상에 단 하나뿐인 사람, 장소, 날짜 등을 나타내는 명사예요. 고유명사의 첫 글자는 항상 대문자로 써요.

Anne, Gilbert, Halla Mountain, Seoul, Canada, January, Friday, Christmas

2. 추상명사는 눈에 보이지 않는 감정이나 생각, 개념 등을 나타내는 명사예요.

love, hope, joy, peace, truth, fear, honesty, music, time, money

3. 물질명사는 액체나 고체, 기체처럼 정해진 형태가 없어 셀 수 없는 물질을 나타내는 명사예요.

water, milk, coffee, bread, gold, paper, sugar, salt, cheese, butter, air, smoke, rain

★ 셀 수 없는 명사에는 a나 an을 붙일 수 없고 복수형으로 쓸 수 없지만, 물질명사는 특별한 단위를 사용하여 수를 나타낼 수 있어요. 물질명사의 복수형은 단위 표현에 -(e)s를 붙여 나타내요.

a cup of **coffee/tea** 커피/차 한 잔	two cups of **coffee/tea** 커피/차 두 잔
a glass of **juice/milk/water** 주스/우유/물 한 잔	two glasses of **juice/milk/water** 주스/우유/물 두 잔
a loaf of **bread** 빵 한 덩어리	two loaves of **bread** 빵 두 덩어리
a piece of **cake/paper** 케이크 한 조각/종이 한 장	two pieces of **cake/paper** 케이크 두 조각/종이 두 장
a slice of **cheese/pizza** 치즈/피자 한 조각	two slices of **cheese/pizza** 치즈/피자 두 조각
a bag of **sugar/fruit** 설탕/과일 한 봉지	two bags of **sugar/fruit** 설탕/과일 두 봉지

> **Tip**
> • cup은 보통 따뜻한 음료, glass는 찬 음료를 담을 때 써요.
> • piece는 큰 덩어리에서 잘라낸 한 조각, slice는 얇고 납작하게 자른 한 조각을 나타내요.

차곡차곡 **기초** 다지기

다음 단어가 해당하는 것에 V표 하세요.

	고유명사	추상명사	물질명사
1. truth			
3. hope			
5. tea			
7. time			

	고유명사	추상명사	물질명사
2. cake			
4. Dorothy			
6. New York			
8. butter			

A 다음 단어들을 셀 수 있는 명사와 셀 수 없는 명사로 구분하여 쓰세요.

brother	Paris	fish	woman	butter	crayon
juice	knife	pig	salt	love	orange

셀 수 있는 명사	셀 수 없는 명사

B 그림을 보고 빈칸에 알맞은 단위 표현을 쓰세요.

1. a _____ of coffee

2. a _____ of sugar

3.  two _____ of paper

4. two _____ of bread

5. a _____ of juice

6. two _____ of cheese

C 다음 문장에서 틀린 부분에 ✕를 표시하고 문장을 고쳐 쓰세요.

1. This is a Daniel. → _____

2. I love musics. → _____

3. My birthday is in march. → _____

4. We drink two cups of milks. → _____

5. He is from spain. → _____

Unit 3 부정관사 a/an

⭐ 관사는 명사 앞에 붙어서 명사가 특정하지 않은 '하나'인지, 정해진 '그' 대상인지 알려주는 역할을 해요. 관사에는 부정관사 a, an과 정관사 the가 있어요.

a pencil
하나의 연필

the pencil
그 연필

⭐ 부정관사 a, an은 특정하지 않은 '하나'를 뜻하며, 셀 수 있는 명사 앞에 붙어요. 자음 소리로 시작하는 단어 앞에는 a, 모음 소리로 시작하는 단어 앞에는 an을 붙여요.

a + 자음 소리로 시작하는 단어	a ball, a car, a monkey, a panda, a store
an + 모음 소리(a, e, i, o, u)로 시작하는 단어	an ant, an egg, an image, an orange, an umbrella

It is a car. 그것은 자동차야.

A panda eats bamboo. 판다는 대나무를 먹어.

It is an ant. 그것은 개미야.

An orange is sweet and sour. 오렌지는 달고 시어.

> **Tip**
> • 셀 수 없는 명사 앞에는 일반적으로 관사를 쓰지 않아요.
>   a love (x) love (o)   a juice (x) a glass of juice (o)   an Oliver (x) Oliver (o)
> • 명사 앞에 다른 형용사가 있는 경우 형용사의 첫 소리에 따라 a나 an을 써요.
>   He is a famous actor. 그는 유명한 배우야.   I have an old shirt. 나는 낡은 셔츠가 있어.

차곡차곡 기초 다지기

부정관사와 명사가 알맞게 쓰이지 않은 구를 모두 찾아 동그라미 하세요.

a train	a onion	a horse
a cat	a butterfly	a airplane
a pen	an kite	an mail
a owl	a truck	a eraser

으쌰으쌰 **실력** 키우기

Ⓐ 다음 중 알맞은 부정관사에 동그라미 하세요. 부정관사가 필요 없으면 ✕에 동그라미 하세요.

1. a   an   ✕   teacher
2. a   an   ✕   alligator
3. a   an   ✕   water

4. a   an   ✕   money
5. a   an   ✕   uncle
6. a   an   ✕   office

7. a   an   ✕   spoon
8. a   an   ✕   love
9. a   an   ✕   lion

Ⓑ 빈칸에 a나 an 중 알맞은 것을 쓰세요.

1. I want to be _____ doctor.

2. The chicken has _____ egg.

3. Thomas is _____ great man.

4. He buys _____ ice cream.

5. It is _____ orange bag.

Ⓒ 그림을 보고 빈칸에 알맞은 부정관사를 쓴 후, 올바른 구에 연결해 문장을 완성하세요.

1.

_____ octopus has •   • slow.

2.

My grandmother is •   • _____ umbrella.

3.

_____ turtle is •   • eight legs.

4.

I have •   • _____ good cook.

Unit 4 정관사 the

 정관사 the는 명사를 특정한 대상으로 정하는 역할을 하며, 보통 '그'라는 뜻으로 쓰여요. 이미 한 번 언급한 명사나 대화를 나누는 사람 모두가 아는 명사 앞에 써요.

I have an apple. <u>The apple</u> is big. 나는 사과가 하나 있어. 그 사과는 커.

Please pass me <u>the salt</u>. 그 소금 좀 주세요.

Tip 정관사 the 뒤에는 자음 소리로 시작하는 명사, 모음 소리로 시작하는 명사, 단수 명사, 복수 명사가 모두 쓰일 수 있어요.

 정관사 the는 다음과 같은 경우에도 써요.

연주하는 악기 이름 앞	play the piano, play the guitar, play the violin
세상에 단 하나밖에 없는 명사 앞	the sun, the moon, the earth, the sky, the galaxy

I play the piano. 나는 피아노를 쳐.   The earth is round. 지구는 둥글어.

 부정관사 a, an이나 정관사 the를 쓰지 않는 경우도 있어요.

운동 경기 이름 앞	soccer, baseball, tennis, basketball
식사 이름 앞	breakfast, lunch, dinner
과목, 언어 이름 앞	math, science, English, Japanese

Kelly plays soccer after school. 켈리는 방과 후에 축구를 해.

I have lunch at twelve. 나는 12시에 점심을 먹어.

He is good at math. 그는 수학을 잘해.

차곡차곡 기초 다지기

다음 중 올바른 표현에 V표 하세요.

1. play cello ☐   play the cello ☐   2. in a sky ☐   in the sky ☐
3. study math ☐   study the math ☐   4. have a dinner ☐   have dinner ☐
5. play tennis ☐   play the tennis ☐   6. speak English ☐   speak an English ☐
7. on moon ☐   on the moon ☐   8. play a violin ☐   play the violin ☐

A 다음을 읽고 알맞은 말에 동그라미 하세요.

1. 정관사 (a | the)는 '그'라는 뜻으로, 특정한 명사를 지칭한다.

2. 세상에 단 하나밖에 없는 명사 앞에는 the를 (붙인다 | 붙이지 않는다).

3. '악기를 연주하다'라고 할 때는 play 뒤에 (a | the)와 악기 이름을 쓴다.

4. 정관사 the는 (처음 언급하는 | 이미 언급한) 명사 앞에 쓴다.

B 빈칸에 정관사가 필요하면 the를, 필요하지 않으면 ✕를 쓰세요.

1. Daniel plays ＿＿＿＿＿＿＿ basketball.

2. ＿＿＿＿＿＿＿ sun makes energy.

3. I have ＿＿＿＿＿＿＿ breakfast every day.

4. I have a dog. ＿＿＿＿＿＿＿ dog is big.

5. Open ＿＿＿＿＿＿＿ door, please.

C 그림을 보고 빈칸에 알맞은 말을 골라 넣어 대화를 완성하세요.

the guitar　　the elephant　　the table　　the sky

1.
   A: Where is my pen?
   B: It is on ＿＿＿＿＿＿ ＿＿＿＿＿＿.

2.
   A: What do you see in ＿＿＿＿＿＿ ＿＿＿＿＿＿?
   B: I see many stars.

3.
   A: Do you play ＿＿＿＿＿＿ ＿＿＿＿＿＿?
   B: Yes, I do.

4.
   A: Look! ＿＿＿＿＿＿ ＿＿＿＿＿＿ is so big.
   B: Wow! It is really big.

꼼꼼하게 종합평가

1. 다음 중 명사를 고르세요.

① read   ② milk   ③ cold

④ sweet   ⑤ hot

2. 다음 중 셀 수 있는 명사를 고르세요.

① love   ② peace   ③ hope

④ pencil   ⑤ honesty

3. 다음 중 셀 수 없는 명사를 고르세요.

① radio   ② woman   ③ violin

④ bag   ⑤ English

4. 다음 중 명사에 대한 설명으로 <u>틀린</u> 것을 고르세요.

① 명사는 사람, 사물, 장소나 개념 등의 이름을 나타낸다.

② 명사는 셀 수 있는 명사와 셀 수 없는 명사로 나눌 수 있다.

③ 명사의 수가 하나일 때 단수, 두 개 이상일 때 복수 라고 한다.

④ 고유명사와 추상명사는 셀 수 있는 명사이다.

⑤ 물질명사는 셀 수 없는 명사이다.

[5~7] 다음 중 복수형이 <u>틀린</u> 것을 고르세요.

5. ① child – children

② mouse – mouses

③ foot – feet

④ box – boxes

⑤ baby – babies

6. ① tooth – teeth

② man – men

③ woman – women

④ tomato – tomatoes

⑤ watch – watchs

7. ① fish – fish

② sheep – sheeps

③ deer – deer

④ cup – cups

⑤ knife – knives

[8~12] a, an, the 중 알맞은 관사를 빈칸에 쓰세요.

8. I have _____ sister.

나는 여동생 한 명이 있다.

9. I see _____ moon every night.

나는 매일 밤 달을 본다.

10. _____ shark is a sea animal.

상어는 바다 동물이다.

11. I see _____ galaxy in the sky.

나는 하늘에서 은하수를 본다.

12. Billy has _____ apple.

빌리는 사과 하나를 가지고 있다.

13. 다음 중 관사에 대한 설명으로 <u>틀린</u> 것을 고르세요.

① 부정관사는 관사가 필요 없을 때 쓴다.

② 부정관사 a, an은 '하나'를 뜻한다.

③ 모음 소리로 시작하는 단어 앞에는 an을 쓴다.

④ 정관사 the는 '그'라는 뜻이 있다.

⑤ 정관사 the는 명사를 특정한 대상으로 정한다.

[14~15] 다음 중 물질명사의 수 표현이 <u>틀린</u> 것을 고르세요.

14. ① a piece of cake
② two slices of cheese
③ a glass of juice
④ two cup of coffee
⑤ a loaf of bread

15. ① two bag of fruits
② two glasses of water
③ three slices of pizza
④ three pieces of paper
⑤ two cups of tea

[16~18] 그림을 보고 빈칸에 알맞은 복수형을 써서 문장을 완성하세요.

16.

The _____ are grey and white.

17.

The boy has three _____.

18.

Six _____ are in the parking lot.

[19~22] 단어를 바르게 배열하여 문장을 완성하세요.

19. 나는 종이 한 장이 필요하다.

| a piece of | paper | I | need |

➡ _____

20. 나는 원숭이 다섯 마리를 본다.

| five | I | monkeys | see |

➡ _____

21. 사랑은 위대하다.

| is | great | Love |

➡ _____

22. 나는 물을 한 잔 마신다.

| drink | water | I | a glass of |

➡ _____

[23~25] 다음 글을 읽고 빈칸에 알맞은 관사를 쓰세요.

Jenny is ²³ _____ student. She likes music. She plays ²⁴ _____ harmonica. It sounds beautiful. She likes to eat ²⁵ _____ orange every day. It is her favorite fruit.

Chapter 03

대명사

Joy 쌤

이번 챕터에서는 대명사에 대해 배울 거야.
대명사는 명사를 대신하는 단어야.

Minho

대신할 대(代) 자를 써서 대명사인가 봐요.

Joy 쌤

 너 한문 많이 아는구나!
대명사에는 '나', '너', '그'처럼 사람의 이름을
대신하는 인칭대명사와 '이것', '저것'처럼
어떤 대상을 가리키는 지시대명사가 있어.

> 인칭대명사: I, you,
> he, she, it, we, they
> 지시대명사: this, that,
> these, those

인칭대명사는 문장에서의 위치와 역할에 따라
주격, 소유격, 목적격, 소유대명사로 모양이
달라져서 특히 잘 알아두어야 해.

Minho

대명사의 종류가 아주 많네요.
이번에도 쉽게 알려주실 거죠?^^

Joy 쌤

당연하지.
걱정하지 말고 대명사 공부 시작해보자!

Unit 1 주격 인칭대명사

⭐ 대명사는 명사를 대신하여 사용하는 단어예요. 인칭대명사는 '나', '너', '그', '그녀', '그것', '우리', '그들'처럼 사람이나 물건의 이름을 대신하는 단어예요.

Joe is my friend. He is nice. 조는 내 친구야. 그는 친절해.

⭐ 문장의 주인공 역할을 하는 주어 대신 쓰는 대명사를 주격 인칭대명사라고 해요. 주격 인칭대명사는 수와 인칭에 따라 달라져요. 말하는 자신은 1인칭, 듣는 상대방은 2인칭, 제삼자는 3인칭이라고 해요.

수	인칭	주격 인칭대명사(~은/는)	문장의 예
단수	1인칭	I 나는	I am Minho. 나는 민호야.
	2인칭	you 너는	You are my sister. 너는 내 여동생이야.
	3인칭	he 그는	He is my brother. 그는 내 남동생이야.
		she 그녀는	She is my teacher. 그녀는 내 선생님이야.
		it 그것은	It is a book. 그것은 책이야.
복수	1인칭	we 우리는	We are students. 우리는 학생이야.
	2인칭	you 너희들은	You are my friends. 너희들은 내 친구들이야.
	3인칭	they 그(것)들은	They are singers. 그들은 가수야.

차곡차곡 기초 다지기

주격 인칭대명사와 뜻을 바르게 연결하세요.

she   he   you(복수)   they   I   it   you(단수)   we

그는   너는   그녀는   우리는   너희들은   그것은   그(것)들은   나는

 실력 키우기

A 알맞은 주격 인칭대명사에 동그라미 하세요.

1. Ms. Grace ➡ she   it
2. you and John ➡ you   they
3. Ben ➡ she   he
4. Andy and Daniel ➡ he   they
5. Emma and I ➡ you   we
6. a boat ➡ it   you
7. animals ➡ they   it
8. my dad ➡ we   he

B 빈칸에 알맞은 주격 인칭대명사를 골라 쓰세요.

1. _____ want this toy.   나는 이 장난감을 원해.

2. _____ play basketball.   그들은 농구를 해.

3. _____ are funny.   너는 재미있어.

4. _____ helps people.   그녀는 사람들을 도와.

5. _____ are Peter and John.   우리는 피터와 존이야.

You
I
We
They
She

C 문장의 주어에 밑줄 친 후, 알맞은 주격 인칭대명사를 쓰세요.

1. Junho is a soccer player. ➡ _____

2. Cats like milk. ➡ _____

3. The camera is new. ➡ _____

4. John and I are from South Africa. ➡ _____

5. The boys and girls play badminton. ➡ _____

Unit 2 소유격 인칭대명사

⭐ 소유격 인칭대명사는 '나의 우산', '너의 책'이라고 할 때의 '나의', '너의'처럼 어떤 대상의 주인을 나타내는 말이에요. 소유격 인칭대명사 뒤에는 항상 명사가 와요.

It is my <u>umbrella</u>. 그것은 내 우산이야.
명사

소유격 인칭대명사는 수와 인칭에 따라 달라져요.

수	인칭	소유격 인칭대명사(~의)	문장의 예
단수	1인칭	my 나의	He is my grandfather. 그는 나의 할아버지야.
	2인칭	your 너의	This is your book. 이것은 너의 책이야.
	3인칭	his 그의	His puppy is cute. 그의 강아지는 귀여워.
		her 그녀의	Her dress is yellow. 그녀의 원피스는 노란색이야.
		its 그것의	The cat plays with its toy. 그 고양이는 자기 장난감을 가지고 놀아.
복수	1인칭	our 우리의	We pack our bags. 우리는 우리의 가방을 싸.
	2인칭	your 너희들의	These are your keys. 이것들은 너희들의 열쇠야.
	3인칭	their 그들의	Their shirts are old. 그들의 셔츠는 낡았어.

차곡차곡 기초 다지기

알맞은 단어를 써서 퍼즐을 완성하세요.

가로

1. 나의
2. 우리의
3. 그들의
4. 그의

세로

5. 그것의
6. 너(희들)의
7. 그녀의

실력 키우기

A 알맞은 소유격 인칭대명사에 동그라미 하세요.

1. it → my its
2. she → her his
3. you(너) → your their
4. I → our my
5. we → our its
6. they → their her
7. you(너희) → his your
8. he → its his

B 소유격 인칭대명사에 동그라미 한 후, 소유격 인칭대명사가 꾸미는 명사에 밑줄 치세요.

(My) grandmother has ten pigs.

1. Your milk is on the table.
2. Mr. Son is our teacher.
3. His box is heavy.
4. Amy and John ride their horses.

C 빈칸에 알맞은 소유격 인칭대명사를 쓰세요.

1. The dog has _____ name. 그 개는 그것의 이름을 가지고 있어.
2. These are _____ cookies. 이것들은 너희들의 쿠키야.
3. _____ umbrella is big. 나의 우산은 커.
4. Bulgogi is _____ favorite food. 불고기는 우리가 가장 좋아하는 음식이야.
5. _____ smile is beautiful. 그녀의 미소는 아름다워.

Unit 3 목적격 인칭대명사

⭐ 문장에서 목적어* 역할을 하는 대명사를 목적격 인칭대명사라고 해요.

<u>Sue</u> is my friend. I like her. 수는 내 친구야. 나는 그녀를 좋아해.

*목적어는 문장에서 주어가 하는 행동의 대상을 나타내요. 목적어는 동사 뒤에 있어요.

목적격 인칭대명사는 수와 인칭에 따라 달라져요.

수	인칭	목적격 인칭대명사(~을/를)	문장의 예
단수	1인칭	me 나를	Mom loves me. 엄마는 나를 사랑해.
	2인칭	you 너를	I like you. 나는 너를 좋아해.
	3인칭	him 그를	I know him. 나는 그를 알아.
		her 그녀를	I help her. 내가 그녀를 도와.
		it 그것을	I want it. 나는 그것을 원해.
복수	1인칭	us 우리를	Dad loves us. 아빠는 우리를 사랑해.
	2인칭	you 너희들을	She knows you. 그녀는 너희들을 알아.
	3인칭	them 그(것)들을	They eat them. 그들은 그것들을 먹어.

 목적격 인칭대명사는 to(~에게), with(~와 함께)와 같은 전치사 뒤에 잘 쓰여요.

Give it <u>to me</u>. 나에게 그것을 줘.   I play <u>with them</u>. 나는 그들과 함께 놀아.

차곡차곡 기초 다지기

목적격 인칭대명사와 뜻을 바르게 연결하세요.

them　　her　　you(단수)　　him　　us　　you(복수)　　it　　me
·　　　·　　　·　　　·　　　·　　　·　　　·　　　·

·　　　·　　　·　　　·　　　·　　　·　　　·　　　·
그를　　나를　　그것을　　너를　　우리를　　그(것)들을　　그녀를　　너희들을

으쌰으쌰 **실력** 키우기

A 다음 주격 인칭대명사를 알맞은 목적격 인칭대명사로 바꿔 쓰세요.

1. you(단수) → _____

2. we → _____

3. he → _____

4. she → _____

5. it → _____

6. they → _____

7. I → _____

8. you(복수) → _____

B 밑줄 친 부분에 알맞은 목적격 인칭대명사를 쓰세요.

1. I remember the story. → _____

2. My father likes my brother and me. → _____

3. She knows Brian. → _____

4. I need you and your friend. → _____

C 그림을 보고 밑줄 친 목적격 인칭대명사에 해당하는 말을 골라 번호를 쓰세요.

① you and me　　② a ball　　③ the teacher　　④ the books

1.  He plays with it. → _____

2.  She reads them. → _____

3.  The students listen to her. → _____

4.  Mom loves us. → _____

Unit 4 소유대명사

⭐ 소유대명사는 <소유격 인칭대명사 + 명사>를 대신하는 인칭대명사예요.

They are <u>my roses</u>. 그것들은 나의 장미야. ➡ They are mine. 그것들은 나의 것이야.
소유격 + 명사

소유대명사는 수와 인칭에 따라 달라져요.

수	인칭	소유격 인칭대명사 + 명사	소유대명사(~의 것)
단수	1인칭	my bag 나의 가방	mine 나의 것
	2인칭	your pencil 너의 연필	yours 너의 것
	3인칭	his cellphone 그의 휴대전화	his 그의 것
		her cat 그녀의 고양이	hers 그녀의 것
복수	1인칭	our house 우리의 집	ours 우리의 것
	2인칭	your shoes 너희들의 신발	yours 너희들의 것
	3인칭	their car 그들의 자동차	theirs 그들의 것

*인칭대명사 it에 해당하는 소유대명사는 없어요.

I have <u>your pencil</u>. 내가 너의 연필을 가지고 있어. ➡ I have yours. 내가 너의 것을 가지고 있어.

It is <u>his cellphone</u>. 그것은 그의 휴대전화야. ➡ It is his. 그것은 그의 것이야.

<u>Their car</u> is red. 그들의 자동차는 빨간색이야. ➡ Theirs is red. 그들의 것은 빨간색이야.

차곡차곡 **기초** 다지기

소유대명사와 뜻을 바르게 연결하세요.

ours　　　　hers　　　yours(단수)　　　theirs　　　　　his　　　　　mine　　　yours(복수)
·　　　　　·　　　　　·　　　　　　·　　　　　·　　　　　·　　　　　·

·　　　　　·　　　　　·　　　　　　·　　　　　·　　　　　·　　　　　·
그녀의 것　　나의 것　　우리의 것　　너희들의 것　　너의 것　　그의 것　　그들의 것

A 다음 주격 인칭대명사를 알맞은 소유대명사로 바꿔 쓰세요.

1. I → _____

2. they → _____

3. she → _____

4. he → _____

5. you(복수) → _____

6. you(단수) → _____

7. we → _____

B 밑줄 친 부분에 알맞은 소유대명사를 쓰세요.

1. They are their birds. → _____

2. Our balloons are big. → _____

3. It is his book. → _____

4. Her dream is nice. → _____

5. Your coat is colorful. → _____

C 빈칸에 알맞은 소유대명사를 쓰세요.

1. The gifts are _____. 그 선물들은 너희들의 것이야.

2. The toys are _____. 그 장난감들은 그의 것이야.

3. Where is _____? 나의 것은 어디 있어?

4. The pictures are _____. 그 그림들은 우리의 것이야.

5. _____ are on the sofa. 그들의 것은 소파 위에 있어.

Unit 5 지시대명사

⭐ 지시대명사는 사람이나 사물을 가리킬 때 쓰는 대명사예요. 가까이 있는 대상을 가리킬 때는 this(이것), 멀리 있는 대상을 가리킬 때는 that(저것)을 써요.

this

that

거리	수	지시대명사	문장의 예
가까이 있는 대상	단수	this 이것, 이 사람	This is a clock. 이것은 시계야.
	복수	these 이것들, 이 사람들	These are rabbits. 이것들은 토끼들이야.
멀리 있는 대상	단수	that 저것, 저 사람	That is the moon. 저것은 달이야.
	복수	those 저것들, 저 사람들	Those are birds. 저것들은 새들이야.

⭐ this, these, that, those는 '이 ~', '저 ~'라는 뜻의 지시형용사로도 쓰여요. 지시형용사로 쓰일 때는 명사 앞에서 명사를 꾸미는 역할을 해요. this와 that 뒤에는 단수 명사가 오고, these와 those 뒤에는 복수 명사가 와요.

This book is interesting.   이 책은 재미있어.

That police car is fast.   저 경찰차는 빨라.

These students are kind.   이 학생들은 친절해.

Those puppies are cute.   저 강아지들은 귀여워.

차곡차곡 **기초** 다지기

다음 단어와 구의 뜻을 찾아 연결하세요.

that •	• 저것들
this •	• 이것들
those •	• 이것
these •	• 저것

this cookie •	• 이 트럭들
those chairs •	• 저 의자들
these trucks •	• 이 쿠키
that store •	• 저 가게

으쌰으쌰 실력 키우기

A 그림을 보고 알맞은 지시대명사를 쓰세요.

1.

2.

3.

4.

_____   _____   _____   _____

B 지시대명사에 동그라미 한 후, 지시대명사가 가리키는 명사구에 밑줄 치세요.

(This) is <u>a piano</u>.

1. That is a desk.

2. This is my mother.

3. These are soccer balls.

4. Those are Sumi's parents.

C 빈칸에 알맞은 말을 골라 넣어 문장을 완성하세요.

1. _____ _____ are tired.
   이 소방관들은 지쳤다.

2. _____ _____ smells nice.
   저 꽃은 좋은 향기가 난다.

3. _____ _____ are hungry.
   저 아기들은 배가 고프다.

4. _____ _____ is yours.
   이 선물은 너의 것이야.

this	babies
that	flower
these	present
those	firefighters

Unit 6 비인칭주어 it

 인칭대명사 it은 사물의 이름을 대신하여 쓰이고, '그것'이라는 뜻이 있어요.

It **is** a tree. 그것은 나무 한 그루야.

I want it. 나는 그것을 원해.

 비인칭주어 it은 날씨, 기온, 요일, 날짜, 시간, 계절, 거리 등을 나타낼 때 주어로 사용되는데 뜻은 없어요. 비인칭주어 it 뒤에는 be동사 is가 쓰여요.

종류	비인칭주어 it과 함께 쓰는 단어의 예	문장의 예
날씨	sunny, windy, rainy, cloudy	It is rainy. 비가 와.
기온	warm, hot, cool, cold	It is cold. 추워.
요일	Sunday, Monday, Tuesday	It is Monday. 월요일이야.
날짜	April 26, December 25	It is April 26. 4월 26일이야.
시간	3 o'clock, ten thirty, 11:45	It is 3 o'clock. 세 시야.
계절	spring, summer, fall, winter	It is spring. 봄이야.
거리	far, near, 3 meters, 5 kilometers	It is 5 kilometers. 5킬로미터야.

Tip 요일과 달은 항상 대문자로 시작해요.

It is Wednesday. 수요일이야.   It is November 27. 11월 27일이야.

 차곡차곡 **기초** 다지기

비인칭주어 it과 함께 쓰는 단어를 모두 찾아 동그라미 하세요.

pencil	sunny	Friday
near	window	10:30
cool	milk	May 31
ring	train	winter

으쌰으쌰 **실력** 키우기

Ⓐ 다음 문장의 it이 무엇에 해당하는지 바르게 연결하세요.

1. It is my puppy. •

인칭대명사 it

3. It is red. •

비인칭주어 it

5. It is July. •

• 2. It is snowy.

• 4. It is hot.

• 6. It is a raincoat.

Ⓑ 단어를 바르게 배열하여 문장을 완성하세요.

1. August 15 / is / it → _____.

2. it / warm / is → _____.

3. 10 meters / it / is → _____.

4. it / summer / is → _____.

5. is / it / one fifteen → _____.

Ⓒ 그림을 보고 빈칸에 알맞은 말을 골라 넣어 대화를 완성하세요.

1.

A: How is the weather?

B: It is _____.

2.

A: What day is it?

B: It is _____.

3.

A: When is your birthday?

B: It is _____.

4.

A: What time is it?

B: It is _____.

December 18
Monday
nine o'clock
cloudy

꼼꼼하게 종합평가

1. 다음 중 대명사가 <u>아닌</u> 것을 고르세요.

① she ② we ③ I
④ they ⑤ Yuna

2. 그림에 알맞은 주격 인칭대명사를 고르세요.

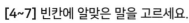

① they ② he
③ it ④ we
⑤ she

3. 그림에 알맞은 목적격 인칭대명사를 고르세요.

① it ② us
③ them ④ her
⑤ him

[4~7] 빈칸에 알맞은 말을 고르세요.

4. _____ is from France.

① She ② Her ③ His
④ Him ⑤ Us

5. I love _____ hometown.

① him ② you ③ my
④ theirs ⑤ it

6. We like _____.

① your ② they ③ its
④ my ⑤ him

7. The book is _____.

① they ② you ③ our
④ mine ⑤ it

[8~9] 그림에 알맞은 지시대명사를 고르세요.

8.

① that ② this ③ these
④ those ⑤ they

9.

① these ② it ③ this
④ that ⑤ those

10. 다음 중 지시대명사의 사용이 <u>틀린</u> 것을 고르세요.

① This is my friend.
② Those are their slippers.
③ These are his pencils.
④ That is her brushes.
⑤ This is our pet.

11. 다음 중 지시형용사의 사용이 바른 것을 고르세요.

① That candies are sour.
② These cat is loud.
③ This cupcake tastes good.
④ Those sock has a hole.
⑤ This teachers are English teachers.

12. 다음 중 문장을 만들 때 비인칭주어 it이 필요하지 <u>않은</u> 것을 고르세요.

① 날씨 ② 요일 ③ 이름
④ 시간 ⑤ 계절

[13~16] 빈칸에 알맞은 말을 쓰세요.

13. _____ is my teddy bear.
저것은 내 곰인형이야.

14. _____ is windy.
바람이 불어.

15. _____ has a red hat.
그녀는 빨간 모자를 가지고 있어.

16. This is _____.
이것은 너의 것이야.

[17~18] 그림을 보고 알맞은 것에 동그라미 하세요.

17.

A: Who is he she ?
B: She is my mine sister.

18.

A: What are these those ?
B: They are egg eggs .

[19~21] 단어를 바르게 배열하여 문장을 완성하세요.

19. 그 집은 그들의 것이야.

 theirs   The house   is

➡ _____

20. 지미는 그것을 좋아해.

 likes   it   Jimmy

➡ _____

21. 그의 가방은 무거워.

 bag   heavy   is   His

➡ _____

[22~25] 다음 글을 읽고 빈칸에 알맞은 대명사를 쓰세요.

Jenny has a little brother. ²² _____(그의) name is Ryan. ²³ _____(그) is 7 years old. She plays with ²⁴ _____(그). Ryan has a soccer ball. It is ²⁵ _____(그의 것).

Chapter 04

be동사

Joy 쌤

이제 be동사에 대해 배울 차례야.
be동사는 동사이지만 움직임을 나타내지 않아.

Minho

동사는 움직임을 나타내는 단어라고 하셨잖아요.
그런데 be동사는 왜 달라요?

Joy 쌤

동사 중에서 be동사는 동작이나 행동을 나타내지 않고,
주어와 다른 단어들을 연결하는 역할을 해.

'그는 학생이다.'라는 문장을 영어로 만들어볼래?

Minho

'그'는 he, '한 명의 학생'이니까
a student, He... a student...

Joy 쌤

이럴 때 be동사를 쓰면 되는 거야.
He와 a student 사이에 be동사 is를 넣으면 돼.

Minho

He is a student. 이렇게요?

Joy 쌤

그래. 이렇게 be동사를 이용해서
문장을 만드는 방법을 알려줄게.

Unit 1 be동사 am, are, is

be동사는 주어와 다른 단어들을 연결하는 역할을 해요. be동사는 주어에 따라 am, are, is로 모양이 달라져요.

주어	be동사	축약형	문장의 예
I	am	I'm	I am a student. 나는 학생이야.
You(단수)	are	You're	You are smart. 너는 똑똑해.
We		We're	We are at the playground. 우리는 놀이터에 있어.
You(복수)		You're	You are mail carriers. 당신들은 우체부들이에요.
They		They're	They are farmers. 그들은 농부들이야.
He	is	He's	He is a pianist. 그는 피아니스트야.
She		She's	She is brave. 그녀는 용감해.
It		It's	It is lovely. 그것은 사랑스러워.

*주어와 be동사는 아포스트로피(')를 써서 줄여 쓸 수 있어요.

be동사는 뒤에 오는 단어에 따라 다르게 해석돼요.

1. 〈주어 + be동사 + 명사〉: 주어와 명사는 같은 존재이며, be동사는 '～이다'라는 뜻이에요.

I am Jake. 나는 제이크야.　Olivia is a teacher. 올리비아는 선생님이야.

2. 〈주어 + be동사 + 형용사〉: 형용사는 주어의 상태를 나타내고, be동사는 '～하다'라는 뜻이에요.

I am happy. 나는 행복해.　The horses are fast. 그 말들은 빨라.

3. 〈주어 + be동사 + 장소를 나타내는 말〉: 주어가 어디에 있는지 알려주며, be동사는 '～에 있다'라는 뜻이에요.

I am at the park. 나는 공원에 있어.　The pen is on the desk. 그 펜은 책상 위에 있어.

차곡차곡 기초 다지기

다음 주어에 알맞은 be동사를 바르게 연결하세요.

We　　　I　　　You　　　He　　　They　　　She　　　It

am　　　are　　　is

A 다음 문장에서 be동사에 동그라미 하세요.

1. You are beautiful.

2. Jenny and I are nurses.

3. Michael is in the classroom.

4. She is funny.

5. I am sleepy.

6. A car is in the parking lot.

B 빈칸에 알맞은 be동사를 쓰세요.

1. He _____ a writer.

2. The flowers _____ fresh.

3. It _____ important.

4. I _____ a dentist.

5. Alice _____ my friend.

6. We _____ on the bus.

C 단어를 바르게 배열하여 문장을 완성하세요.

1. is / it / a bird → _____
   그것은 새야.

2. my sisters / in Florida / are → _____
   내 언니들은 플로리다에 있어.

3. I / a pilot / am → _____
   나는 비행기 조종사야.

4. is / Julia / kind → _____
   줄리아는 친절해.

Unit 2 be동사 긍정문과 부정문

 be동사 긍정문은 <주어 + be동사 + ~> 형태의 문장으로, '~이다', '~하다', '~에 있다'라는 뜻을 나타내요.

He is a cashier. 그는 계산원이야.

I am excited. 나는 신이 나.

They are at the zoo. 그들은 동물원에 있어.

be동사 부정문은 be동사 뒤에 not이 들어간 문장으로, '~이 아니다'라는 부정의 뜻이 있어요.

주어	be동사	축약형	문장의 예
I	am not	없음	I am not a lawyer. 나는 변호사가 아니야.
You(단수) We You(복수) They	are not	aren't	You are not alone. 너는 혼자가 아니야. We are not old. 우리는 늙지 않았어. You are not musicians. 너희들은 음악가들이 아니야. They are not lazy. 그들은 게으르지 않아.
He She It	is not	isn't	He is not a baseball player. 그는 야구 선수가 아니야. She is not tall. 그녀는 키가 크지 않아. It is not in my pocket. 그것은 내 주머니에 없어.

Tip <주어 + be동사 + not>은 다음과 같이 줄여서 쓸 수도 있어요.

I am not ➡ I'm not

You are not ➡ You're not   We are not ➡ We're not   They are not ➡ They're not

He is not ➡ He's not   She is not ➡ She's not   It is not ➡ It's not

차곡차곡 **기초** 다지기

다음 주어에 알맞은 be동사의 부정형을 바르게 연결하세요.

They   You   She   It   We   I   He

am not   are not   is not

Ⓐ 다음 중 알맞은 것에 동그라미 하세요.

1. We is are at the museum.   2. It isn't aren't rainy.

3. The garden is are beautiful.   4. I isn't am not an artist.

5. Mr. Simon isn't aren't tall.   6. They am are good friends.

Ⓑ 다음 긍정문은 부정문으로, 부정문은 긍정문으로 바꿔 쓰세요.

1. We are in France.   → _____

2. They are not chocolate cookies.   → _____

3. I am cold.   → _____

4. It is not difficult.   → _____

Ⓒ 그림을 보고 단어를 바르게 배열하여 문장을 완성하세요.

1.   my sister / sick / is

   → _____

2.  aren't / a singer / you

   → _____

3.  the backpack / on the desk / isn't

   → _____

4.  am / I / busy

   → _____

Unit 3 be동사 의문문

★ be동사 의문문은 be동사로 시작하는 질문이에요. be동사 긍정문에서 주어와 be동사의 자리를 바꿔 be동사를 문장 맨 앞으로 옮기고 마지막에 물음표를 쓰면 be동사 의문문이 완성돼요.

She is Mary. 그녀는 메리야. ➡ Is she Mary? 그녀는 메리니?

be동사	주어	문장의 예
Am	I	Am I late? 제가 늦었나요?
Are	you(단수) we you(복수) they	Are you a student? 너는 학생이니? Are we in Seoul? 우리는 서울에 있나요? Are you Rosie and Daniel? 너희들이 로지와 다니엘이니? Are they okay? 그들은 괜찮니?
Is	he she it	Is he Jisung? 그가 지성이니? Is she Korean? 그녀는 한국인이니? Is it a watermelon? 그것은 수박이니?

★ be동사 의문문에 대한 대답은 다음과 같아요.

be동사 의문문	긍정 대답	부정 대답
Am I …?	Yes, you are.	No, you aren't.
Are you …? Are we …? Are you …? Are they …?	Yes, I am. Yes, you/we are. Yes, we are. Yes, they are.	No, I'm not. No, you/we aren't. No, we aren't. No, they aren't.
Is he …? Is she …? Is it …?	Yes, he is. Yes, she is. Yes, it is.	No, he isn't. No, she isn't. No, it isn't.

차곡차곡 **기초** 다지기

다음에 알맞은 의문문 형태를 쓰세요.

1. I am ➡ _____ ? 　　2. He is ➡ _____ ?

3. You are ➡ _____ ? 　　4. It is ➡ _____ ?

5. We are ➡ _____ ? 　　6. They are ➡ _____ ?

 실력 키우기

A 다음 중 알맞은 것에 동그라미 하세요.

1. Are they   Is it   her brothers?

2. Are you   Are we   a police officer?

3. Are they   Is she   Angela?

4. Is it   Am I   a comic book?

5. Am I   Are they   penguins?

6. Is he   Is she   your dad?

B 다음 문장을 의문문으로 바꿔 쓰세요.

1. You are a soccer player.   ➔ _____

2. The movie is boring.   ➔ _____

3. They are gorillas.   ➔ _____

4. John is a good boy.   ➔ _____

C 그림을 보고 빈칸에 알맞은 단어를 골라 넣어 대화를 완성하세요.

he   yes   you   isn't   are   is   not   it

1.

A: Are _____ at the playground?

B: No, I'm _____ .

2.

A: _____ he your grandfather?

B: Yes, _____ is.

3.

A: _____ they Chinese?

B: _____ , they are.

4.

A: Is _____ rainy?

B: No, it _____ .

1. 다음 중 be동사에 대한 설명으로 **틀린** 것을 고르세요.

① be동사의 종류로는 am, are, is가 있다.
② be동사는 움직임을 나타내지 않는다.
③ be동사 긍정문에는 not이 들어가지 않는다.
④ be동사 의문문은 명사로 시작한다.
⑤ be동사 부정문에는 not이 들어간다.

[2~3] 밑줄 친 be동사가 바르게 쓰인 문장을 고르세요.

2. ① You <u>is</u> wonderful.
② She <u>are</u> a girl.
③ It <u>am</u> sweet.
④ They <u>are</u> honest.
⑤ I <u>is</u> in the bed.

3. ① We <u>am</u> in Italy.
② It <u>is</u> an interesting story.
③ They <u>is</u> Americans.
④ I <u>are</u> in the kitchen.
⑤ He <u>are</u> very nice.

4. 다음 중 be동사 부정문으로 바른 것을 고르세요.

① She are not from Texas.
② They isn't funny.
③ Jake is not small.
④ I aren't tired.
⑤ We aren't a pianist.

5. 다음 중 be동사 의문문으로 바른 것을 고르세요.

① Are she Sarah?
② Is it your cellphone?
③ Am we on the mountain?
④ Is he guitarists?
⑤ Am they strong?

[6~10] 다음 중 알맞은 것에 동그라미 하세요.

6. Is Are you ready?

7. Jessica aren't isn't from Germany.

8. The babies am are twins.

9. I is am not perfect.

10. Am Is it yours?

[11~14] 다음 보기 중 질문에 알맞은 대답을 고르세요.

① Yes, he is.　　② No, it isn't.
③ No, I'm not.　　④ Yes, they are.

11. A: Is it windy?
B: (　　　　)

12. A: Are they dolphins?
B: (　　　　)

13. A: Are you at the library?
B: (　　　　)

14. A: Is he friendly?
B: (　　　　)

[15~19] 단어를 바르게 배열하여 문장을 완성하세요.

15. 그는 화났어.

| is | angry | He |

➜ _____

16. 새들이 나무 위에 앉아 있니?

| the birds | on the tree | Are |

➜ _____

17. 너는 못생기지 않았어.

| aren't | You | ugly |

➜ _____

18. 그녀는 아프지 않아.

| She | sick | is | not |

➜ _____

19. 그 책은 지루하니?

| Is | boring | the book |

➜ _____

[20~21] 그림을 보고 알맞은 것에 동그라미 하세요.

20.

A: Jake, is are you hungry?

B: Yes No , I'm not. I'm very full.

21.

A: Is Are it a ladybug?

B: Yes, it she is.

[22~25] 다음 글을 읽고 빈칸에 알맞은 be동사를 쓰세요.

It ²² _____ Jenny's birthday today. Her grandparents ²³ _____ at Jenny's house. The birthday cake ²⁴ _____ on the table. Is she eleven years old? No, she ²⁵ _____ She is twelve years old.

Chapter 05

일반동사

Joy 쌤

Hey, Minho. Are you there?

Minho

Yes, I'm here.
오늘은 어떤 걸 알려주실 거예요?

Joy 쌤

'먹는다', '잔다', '논다', '공부하다' 이런 단어들의
공통점이 뭔지 아니?

Minho

음, 모두 행동을 알려주는 단어예요. 동사 맞죠?!

Joy 쌤

You're right. 동사 맞아. 이번 챕터에서는
움직임을 나타내는 일반동사가 쓰인 문장들을 배울 거야.

I teach English.
이 문장에서 동사가 뭘까?

Minho

동사는 주어 다음에 온다고 했으니까 teach예요.
그럼 여기서 동사는 뭘까요? I study English.

Joy 쌤

동사는 study야. 대단한데?! 그럼 본격적으로 시작해보자.

Unit 1 일반동사 현재형

⭐ 모든 문장에는 동사가 있어요. 동사는 문장에서 주인공이 어떤 행동을 하는지 알려주는 역할을 해요. 주로 상태를 나타내는 be동사와 달리 일반동사는 움직임을 나타내요.

I study English. 나는 영어를 공부해.

We eat lunch at 12 o'clock. 우리는 12시에 점심을 먹어.

⭐ 일반동사 현재형은 현재의 사실, 습관이나 취향, 일반적인 사실을 말할 때 사용해요. 문장에서 동사는 보통 주어의 바로 뒤에 위치해요.

I live in London. 나는 런던에 살아. (현재의 사실)

I go to school every day. 나는 매일 학교에 가. (습관/취향)

The sun rises in the east. 해는 동쪽에서 떠. (일반적인 사실)

⭐ 주어가 3인칭 단수(he, she, it, Tony, the dog 등)인 문장에서는 일반동사 뒤에 -s나 -es를 붙여요.

대부분의 동사	+ -s	like ➡ likes, read ➡ reads, play ➡ plays
s, ch, sh, o로 끝나는 동사	+ -es	dress ➡ dresses, catch ➡ catches, brush ➡ brushes, go ➡ goes, do ➡ does
'자음 + y'로 끝나는 동사	y ➡ i + -es	cry ➡ cries, fly ➡ flies, study ➡ studies
불규칙적으로 변하는 동사		have ➡ has

He reads a book. 그는 책을 읽어.　　　　　She brushes her teeth. 그녀는 이를 닦아.

It has a long neck. 그것은 긴 목을 가지고 있어.　　Tony does his homework. 토니는 숙제를 해.

차곡차곡 기초 다지기

다음 중 일반동사를 모두 찾아 동그라미 하세요.

scissors	cellphone	eat	money
sleep	cheese	walk	am
paper	smile	study	lamp
play	are	talk	is

A 다음 문장에서 일반동사에 동그라미 하세요.

1. Julie draws a picture.
2. I listen to the radio.
3. The children drink milk.
4. Turtles move slowly.
5. He waters the garden.
6. We bake blueberry muffins.

B 빈칸에 알맞은 일반동사를 골라 알맞은 형태로 고쳐 쓰세요.

go　　study　　have　　travel　　meet　　wash

1. The girl _____ her hands.　그 소녀는 손을 씻는다.
2. Paul _____ new people.　폴은 새로운 사람들을 만난다.
3. Harry _____ the world.　해리는 세계를 여행한다.
4. Lily _____ math.　릴리는 수학을 공부한다.
5. Tom _____ to the library.　톰은 도서관에 간다.
6. The restaurant _____ milk shake.　그 식당에는 밀크셰이크가 있다.

C 단어를 바르게 배열하여 문장을 완성하세요.

1. honey / bees / make　→ _____
　　　　　　　　　　　　　　벌들은 꿀을 만든다.

2. Mary / a little lamb / has　→ _____
　　　　　　　　　　　　　　메리는 작은 어린양을 가지고 있다.

3. coffee / my mom / drinks　→ _____
　　　　　　　　　　　　　　우리 엄마는 커피를 마신다.

4. watches / a movie / Derek　→ _____
　　　　　　　　　　　　　　데렉은 영화를 본다.

Unit 2 일반동사 부정문

⭐ 일반동사 부정문은 주어에 따라 do not이나 does not을 일반동사 앞에 넣어서 만들어요. do not 또는 does not 뒤에는 항상 동사원형이 와요.

I like chocolate. 나는 초콜릿을 좋아해. ➡ I do not like chocolate. 나는 초콜릿을 좋아하지 않아.

He plays baseball. 그는 야구를 해. ➡ He does not play baseball. 그는 야구를 하지 않아.

주어	do/does + not	문장의 예
I	do not (= don't)	I don't like cold weather. 나는 추운 날씨를 좋아하지 않아.
you(단수) we you(복수) they	do not (= don't)	You don't understand me. 너는 나를 이해하지 못해. We don't live in Seoul. 우리는 서울에 살지 않아. You don't eat vegetables. 너희들은 야채를 먹지 않는구나. They don't wear glasses. 그들은 안경을 쓰지 않아.
He She It	does not (= doesn't)	He doesn't go to school. 그는 학교에 가지 않아. She doesn't take a bus. 그녀는 버스를 타지 않아. It doesn't work. 그것은 작동되지 않아.

Tip 주어가 복수 명사이면 don't, 단수 명사이면 doesn't를 써요.
<u>My parents</u> <u>don't</u> like fishing. 우리 부모님은 낚시를 좋아하지 않으셔.
<u>The cheese</u> <u>doesn't</u> taste good. 그 치즈는 맛이 좋지 않아.

차곡차곡 기초 다지기

다음 주어에 알맞은 일반동사의 부정형을 바르게 연결하세요.

We   Her friends   He   The lady   I   A donut

don't   doesn't

The dog   They   Jay and I   Samuel   She   It

A 다음 중 알맞은 것에 동그라미 하세요.

1. She   don't   doesn't   eat peaches.

2. I   don't   doesn't   watch scary movies.

3. He   do not   does not   play the guitar.

4. They   do not   does not   learn Spanish.

B 다음 긍정문은 부정문으로, 부정문은 긍정문으로 바꿔 쓰세요.

1. I don't know her name.   → _____

2. Suyeon buys toys.   → _____

3. The girls don't jump on the bed.   → _____

4. The train stops at the station.   → _____

C 그림을 보고 단어를 바르게 배열하여 문장을 완성하세요.

1.    teach / doesn't / she / math

   → _____

2.   speak / don't / loudly / we

   → _____

3.   the grasshopper / work / doesn't

   → _____

4.    the boy / look / doesn't / good

   → _____

Unit 3 일반동사 의문문

 일반동사 의문문은 Do나 Does로 문장을 시작하고, 문장 끝에는 물음표를 붙여요. 일반동사 부정문과 마찬가지로 Do나 Does 뒤에는 항상 동사원형이 와요.

You like carrots. 너는 당근을 좋아해. ➡ Do you like carrots? 너 당근 좋아하니?

He likes music. 그는 음악을 좋아해. ➡ Does he like music? 그는 음악을 좋아하니?

Do/Does	주어	문장의 예
Do	I	Do I look okay? 나 괜찮아 보여?
Do	you(단수) we you(복수) they	Do you like this book? 너는 이 책을 좋아하니? Do we need crayons? 우리는 크레용이 필요할까? Do you know Minsu? 너희들 민수 아니? Do they play the piano? 그들은 피아노를 연주하니?
Does	he she it	Does he remember you? 그는 너를 기억하니? Does she eat Bulgogi? 그녀는 불고기를 먹니? Does it work? 그것은 작동하니?

 일반동사 의문문에 대한 대답은 다음과 같아요.

일반동사 의문문	긍정 대답	부정 대답
Do I ...?	Yes, you do.	No, you don't.
Do you ...? Do we ...? Do you ...? Do they ...?	Yes, I do. Yes, you/we do. Yes, we do. Yes, they do.	No, I don't. No, you/we don't. No, we don't. No, they don't.
Does he ...? Does she ...? Does it ...?	Yes, he does. Yes, she does. Yes, it does.	No, he doesn't. No, she doesn't. No, it doesn't.

차곡차곡 기초 다지기

다음에 알맞은 의문문 형태를 쓰세요.

1. He has ➡ _____?
2. It starts ➡ _____?
3. You drive ➡ _____?
4. The man fixes ➡ _____?
5. They carry ➡ _____?
6. The kids play ➡ _____?

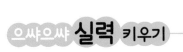

으쌰으쌰 실력 키우기

A 다음 문장을 의문문으로 바꿔 쓰세요.

1. The bakery makes cakes. ➡ _____

2. You swim in the morning. ➡ _____

3. The sun sets in the evening. ➡ _____

4. The giraffe eats grass. ➡ _____

B 밑줄 친 부분을 고쳐서 문장을 다시 쓰세요.

1. Do you <u>speaks</u> English? ➡ _____

2. <u>Does</u> they trust him? ➡ _____

3. Does he <u>has</u> a sore throat? ➡ _____

4. <u>Does</u> the fruits smell good? ➡ _____

C 그림을 보고 빈칸에 알맞은 단어를 골라 넣어 대화를 완성하세요.

he   do   they   does   she   don't   yes   doesn't

1.

A: _____ you see a pig?
B. No, I _____. I see a rabbit.

2.

A: Does _____ like the toy?
B: Yes, he _____.

3.

A: Do _____ play badminton?
B: _____, they do.

4.

A: Does _____ eat vegetables?
B: No, she _____.

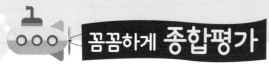

1. 다음 중 일반동사 현재형에 대한 설명으로 바른 것을 고르세요.
   ① 일반동사 현재형은 am, are, is이다.
   ② 일반동사 현재형에서 동사는 움직임을 나타낸다.
   ③ 일반동사 현재형은 부정문으로 쓸 수 없다.
   ④ 일반동사 현재형의 의문은 be동사로 시작한다.
   ⑤ 일반동사 현재형에서 he, she, it이 주어일 때는 동사 뒤에 -s를 붙이지 않는다.

2. 다음 중 일반동사의 쓰임이 바른 문장을 고르세요.
   ① Mike drink milk.
   ② We loves our dog.
   ③ The rabbit run fast.
   ④ Olivia travels to Korea.
   ⑤ They swims in the swimming pool.

3. 다음 중 일반동사 부정문으로 바른 것을 고르세요.
   ① I doesn't work on Monday.
   ② Bill and Sue don't teach English.
   ③ She don't catch a ball.
   ④ You doesn't listen to me.
   ⑤ My father don't like eggplant.

4. 다음 중 일반동사 의문문으로 바른 것을 고르세요.
   ① Does Paul drives a car?
   ② Do Jenny answer the phone?
   ③ Do you plays the piano?
   ④ Does your dog likes you?
   ⑤ Do they listen to K-pop?

[5~7] 다음 문장을 부정문으로 바꿔 쓰세요.

5. The class finishes at 12.

   ➜ _____

6. They wear uniforms.

   ➜ _____

7. Jake lives in Korea.

   ➜ _____

[8~10] 다음 문장을 의문문으로 바꿔 쓰세요.

8. You like the story.

   ➜ _____

9. A doctor helps sick people.

   ➜ _____

10. Your friends like swimming.

    ➜ _____

[11~14] 다음 보기 중 질문에 알맞은 대답을 고르세요.

① Yes, I do.   ② No, they don't.
③ Yes, she does.   ④ Yes, it does.

11. A: Do you eat eggs?
    B: (   )

12. A: Does Amy keep a diary?

    B: (   )

13. A: Do birds live in water?

    B: (   )

14. A: Does the dog feel soft?

    B: (   )

[15~19] 다음 문장에서 <u>틀린</u> 부분을 찾아 바르게 고쳐 쓰세요.

15. I finishes my homework in the evening.

    ➡ _____

16. The farmer feed the animals.

    ➡ _____

17. Lemons doesn't taste sweet.

    ➡ _____

18. We dances at the party.

    ➡ _____

19. Sally ride a bicycle.

    ➡ _____

[20~21] 그림을 보고 알맞은 것에 동그라미 하세요.

20.

A: Do Does you like your new dress?

B: Yes No , I do. It is pretty.

21.

A: Do Does he have an umbrella?

B: No, he don't doesn't .

[22~25] 다음 글을 읽고 괄호 안의 단어를 알맞은 형태로 고쳐 쓰세요.

Jenny's grandmother [22] _____ (bake) homemade cookies for Jenny and her brother. Jenny [23] _____ (help) her grandmother. Jenny's brother [24] _____ (don't) help his grandmother. However, he eats some cookies later. [25] _____ (Do) the grandmother like him? Of course, she does.

*homemade 집에서 만든, 손으로 만든
*of course 물론

Chapter 06

시제

꼼꼼하게 종합평가

Joy 쌤

이번 챕터에서는 문장의 시제에 대해 배울 거야.
시제는 크게 현재, 과거, 미래로 나눌 수 있어.

자, 여기서 퀴즈!
'나는 축구를 한다.' 이 문장을 과거형으로 어떻게 말할까?

Minho

'나는 축구를 했다.' 맞죠?!

Joy 쌤

그렇지!
나는 축구를 한다. (현재)
나는 축구를 하고 있다. (현재진행)
나는 축구를 했다. (과거)
나는 축구를 할 것이다. (미래)
어때, 쉽지?

Minho

동사만 시제에 맞게 바꿔 쓰면 되니까
어렵지 않을 것 같아요.

Joy 쌤

맞아. 어렵지 않아. 자세히 알려줄게!

현재진행형은 주어가 지금 하고 있는 일을 나타낼 때 사용해요. <be동사 + 동사원형-ing> 형태로 쓰며, '~하고 있다'라는 뜻이에요.

주어	현재진행형	문장의 예
I	am 동사원형-ing	I am studying English. 나는 영어를 공부하고 있어.
You We They	are 동사원형-ing	You are riding a swing. 너는/너희들은 그네를 타고 있어. We are having dinner. 우리는 저녁을 먹고 있어. They are running. 그들은 달리고 있어.
He She It	is 동사원형-ing	He is playing soccer. 그는 축구를 하고 있어. She is taking pictures. 그녀는 사진을 찍고 있어. It is catching a ball. 그것은 공을 잡고 있어.

Tip 보통 동사 뒤에 -ing를 붙이지만, e로 끝나는 동사는 e를 없애고 -ing를 붙이고, '단모음 + 단자음'으로 끝나는 동사는 자음을 한 번 더 쓰고 -ing를 붙여요.

skate ➡ skating, ride ➡ riding, have ➡ having, run ➡ running, stop ➡ stopping

현재진행형의 부정문은 be동사 뒤에 not을 붙이며, '~하고 있지 않다'라는 뜻이에요.

I am not watching TV. 나는 TV를 보고 있지 않아.

We are not drawing a picture. 우리는 그림을 그리고 있지 않아.

현재진행형의 의문문은 be동사를 문장 맨 앞으로 보내고 문장 끝에 물음표를 붙여요. '~하고 있니?'라는 뜻이에요.

Are you brushing your teeth? 너 이 닦고 있니?

Is Jane sleeping? 제인은 자고 있니?

Tip 현재진행형의 의문문에 대한 대답은 be동사 의문문의 대답과 같아요.
Are they singing? 그들은 노래하고 있니? ➡ Yes, they are. / No, they aren't.

차곡차곡 **기초** 다지기

다음 동사를 '동사원형-ing' 형태로 바꿔 쓰세요.

1. drive ➡ _____

2. read ➡ _____

3. stop ➡ _____

4. come ➡ _____

5. wash ➡ _____

6. swim ➡ _____

A 빈칸에 알맞은 동사를 골라 현재진행형으로 바꿔 쓰세요.

1. I ＿＿＿＿＿＿＿＿ ＿＿＿＿＿＿＿ a letter.

2. He ＿＿＿＿＿＿＿＿ ＿＿＿＿＿＿＿ on the phone.

3. We ＿＿＿＿＿＿＿＿ ＿＿＿＿＿＿＿ a cake.

4. The children ＿＿＿＿＿＿＿ ＿＿＿＿＿＿＿ a song.

bake

sing

write

talk

B 다음 긍정문을 부정문으로 바꿔 쓰세요.

1. They are watching a movie.　→ ＿＿＿＿＿＿＿＿＿＿＿＿＿＿＿＿＿＿＿

2. The boy is doing his homework.　→ ＿＿＿＿＿＿＿＿＿＿＿＿＿＿＿＿＿＿＿

3. I am traveling to New York.　→ ＿＿＿＿＿＿＿＿＿＿＿＿＿＿＿＿＿＿＿

4. They are kicking balls.　→ ＿＿＿＿＿＿＿＿＿＿＿＿＿＿＿＿＿＿＿

C 그림을 보고 질문에 알맞은 대답을 쓰세요.

1.

A: Is it raining?

B: ＿＿＿＿＿, ＿＿＿＿＿ ＿＿＿＿＿. It is snowing.

2.

A: Is your sister playing computer games?

B: ＿＿＿＿＿, ＿＿＿＿＿ ＿＿＿＿＿. She's reading a book.

3.

A: Are you riding a bike?

B: ＿＿＿＿＿, ＿＿＿＿＿ ＿＿＿＿＿.

4.

A: Are they dancing?

B: ＿＿＿＿＿, ＿＿＿＿＿ ＿＿＿＿＿.

Unit 2 be동사 과거형

be동사 과거형은 과거의 주어의 상태를 나타내며, '~이었다, ~ 있었다'라는 뜻이에요. 주어가 단수일 때는 was, 복수일 때는 were를 써요.

주어	현재형	과거형	문장의 예
I	am	was	I was happy. 나는 행복했어.
You / We / They	are	were	You were a baby. 너는 아기였어. They were my teachers. 그들은 나의 선생님이셨어.
He / She / It	is	was	He was at school. 그는 학교에 있었어. It was heavy. 그것은 무거웠어.

be동사 과거형의 부정문은 be동사 과거형 뒤에 not을 붙이며, '~이 아니었다, ~ 없었다'라는 뜻이에요.

I was not thirsty. 나는 목마르지 않았어.   You were not at home. 너는 집에 없었어.

Tip was not은 wasn't로, were not은 weren't로 줄여 쓸 수 있어요.

be동사 과거형의 의문문은 be동사 과거형을 문장 맨 앞으로 보내고 문장 끝에 물음표를 붙여요. '~이었니?, ~ 있었니?'라는 뜻이에요.

Was Megan sick? 메간이 아팠니?   Were they at the playground? 그들은 놀이터에 있었니?

Tip be동사 과거형의 의문문에 대한 대답은 긍정이면 〈Yes, 주어 + was/were.〉, 부정이면 〈No, 주어 + wasn't/weren't.〉로 써요.

Were you tired? 너는 피곤했니? ➡ Yes, I was. / No, I wasn't.

차곡차곡 기초 다지기

다음 주어에 알맞은 be동사의 과거형과 과거 부정형을 쓰세요.

	be동사 과거형	be동사 과거 부정형		be동사 과거형	be동사 과거 부정형
1. Cathy	_____	_____	2. They	_____	_____
3. The store	_____	_____	4. We	_____	_____
5. You	_____	_____	6. I	_____	_____
7. She	_____	_____	8. Scott	_____	_____

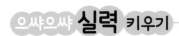

A 빈칸에 was와 were 중 알맞은 것을 쓰세요.

1. The turtle _____ slow.   2. They _____ noisy.

3. I _____ not sad.   4. The birds _____ in the nest.

5. She _____ late for school.   6. I _____ sick yesterday.

7. We _____ not tired.   8. He _____ at the bus stop.

B 다음 긍정문을 괄호 안의 형태에 맞게 바꿔 쓰세요.

1. She was hungry.   → _____ (부정문)

2. He was a soccer player.   → _____ (의문문)

3. They were nice.   → _____ (부정문)

4. The trip was fun.   → _____ (의문문)

C 그림을 보고 빈칸에 알맞은 말을 써서 대화를 완성하세요.

1.    A: Were you a firefighter?
   B: Yes, _____ _____.

2.    A: Was the cat in the room?
   B: _____, _____ wasn't. It was on the lawn.

3.    A: Was he in the classroom?
   B: No, he _____. He _____ in the playground.

4.    A: Were they happy?
   B: _____, they _____.

Unit 3 일반동사 과거형

일반동사 과거형은 주어가 과거에 어떤 행동을 했는지를 나타내요. 일반동사 과거형은 '~했다'라는 뜻으로, 대부분 동사원형에 -ed를 붙여요.

대부분의 동사	+ -ed	play ➡ played, brush ➡ brushed, point ➡ pointed, talk ➡ talked
e로 끝나는 동사	+ -d	live ➡ lived, love ➡ loved, like ➡ liked, close ➡ closed, change ➡ changed
'모음 + 자음'으로 끝나는 동사	+ 마지막 자음 + -ed	plan ➡ planned, drop ➡ dropped, stop ➡ stopped, hug ➡ hugged
'자음 + y'로 끝나는 동사	y ➡ i + -ed	cry ➡ cried, study ➡ studied, carry ➡ carried, dry ➡ dried

I played badminton with my dad. 나는 아빠와 배드민턴을 쳤어.

Erin studied science. 에린은 과학을 공부했어.

 일반동사 과거형은 인칭이나 수에 관계없이 형태가 같아요.

He moved to Daejeon. 그는 대전으로 이사했어.　　They moved to a new house. 그들은 새집으로 이사했어.

일반동사 과거형에는 -ed를 붙이는 규칙을 따르지 않는 동사가 많이 있어요.

go ➡ went	write ➡ wrote	sit ➡ sat	have ➡ had
make ➡ made	do ➡ did	read ➡ read	speak ➡ spoke
see ➡ saw	eat ➡ ate	cut ➡ cut	give ➡ gave
meet ➡ met	take ➡ took	run ➡ ran	sleep ➡ slept

I wrote a letter to my uncle. 나는 삼촌에게 편지를 썼어.

We saw many animals in the zoo. 우리는 동물원에서 많은 동물들을 보았어.

▶ 더 많은 불규칙 동사 변화는 p.148을 참고하세요.

차곡차곡 **기초** 다지기

다음 일반동사의 과거형을 쓰세요.

1. work ➡ _____

2. write ➡ _____

3. go ➡ _____

4. cry ➡ _____

5. use ➡ _____

6. stop ➡ _____

으쌰으쌰 **실력** 키우기

Ⓐ 다음 현재형 문장의 동사에 밑줄 친 후, 과거형으로 고쳐 쓰세요.

1. I study math.   → _____

2. Randy plays the piano.   → _____

3. We eat dinner at 6 o'clock.   → _____

4. Sarah orders an ice cream.   → _____

5. They see a deer.   → _____

6. The students read the book in the library. → _____

Ⓑ 빈칸에 알맞은 단어를 골라 넣어 문장을 완성하세요.

asked   smiled   shared   ran

1. We _____ at the baby.   우리는 그 아기를 보고 미소 지었다.

2. The children _____ the snack.   그 아이들은 간식을 나눠먹었다.

3. She _____ to the school.   그녀는 학교로 달려갔다.

4. Adam _____ a question.   아담은 질문을 했다.

Ⓒ 단어를 바르게 배열하여 문장을 완성하세요.

1. dropped / Jim / the vase   → _____
                                      짐은 꽃병을 떨어뜨렸다.

2. they / to Mexico / traveled   → _____
                                      그들은 멕시코로 여행을 갔다.

3. cleaned / the room / Amy   → _____
                                      에이미는 방을 청소했다.

4. sick / felt / he   → _____
                                      그는 아팠다.

Unit 4 일반동사 과거형 부정문과 의문문

⭐ 일반동사 과거형 부정문은 주어가 과거에 어떤 행동을 하지 않았다는 것을 나타내는 문장이에요. 일반동사 현재형 부정문에서 주어에 따라 do not이나 does not을 썼다면, 일반동사 과거형 부정문에서는 주어에 관계없이 did not을 일반동사 원형 앞에 붙여요.

현재 I do not play soccer.
나는 축구를 하지 않아.

He does not drink milk.
그는 우유를 마시지 않아.

과거 I did not play soccer.
나는 축구를 하지 않았어.

He did not drink milk.
그는 우유를 마시지 않았어.

 did not은 didn't로 줄여 쓸 수 있어요.
We <u>didn't</u> buy apples. 우리는 사과를 사지 않았어.

⭐ 일반동사 과거형 의문문은 주어가 과거에 어떤 행동을 했는지 묻는 문장이에요. 일반동사 과거형 의문문은 Did를 문장 맨 앞에 넣고 문장 끝에 물음표를 붙여요.

Did you wash your hands? 너는 손을 씻었니?
Did she like the cookies? 그녀가 그 쿠키를 좋아했니?
Did they go shopping? 그들은 쇼핑하러 갔니?

 • 일반동사 과거형 긍정문을 의문문으로 만들 때 과거형 동사는 동사원형으로 바꾸어요.
You <u>finished</u> your homework. ➡ Did you <u>finish</u> your homework?
너는 숙제를 끝냈어. 너는 숙제를 끝냈니?

• 일반동사 과거형 의문문에 대한 대답은 긍정이면 〈Yes, 주어 + did.〉, 부정이면 〈No, 주어 + didn't.〉로 써요.
Did you visit your grandparents? 너는 할아버지댁을 방문했니? ➡ Yes, I did. / No, I didn't.

차곡차곡 기초 다지기

일반동사 과거형의 부정문과 의문문 형태가 바르면 ○에, 틀리면 ✕에 V표 하세요.

1. We didn't have fun.   ○ ✕
2. Did he buys a cake? ○ ✕
3. You didn't played tennis.   ○ ✕
4. I didn't wear a hat.   ○ ✕
5. Did it rains?   ○ ✕
6. Did she ride a bike? ○ ✕
7. Beth didn't help Max.   ○ ✕
8. Did they slept well? ○ ✕

으쌰으쌰 **실력** 키우기

A 괄호 안의 단어를 사용해 일반동사 과거형 부정문을 완성하세요.

1. The boy _____ _____ his hair. (brush)

2. They _____ _____ their best. (try)

3. I _____ _____ my room. (clean)

4. We _____ _____ the answer. (know)

B 다음 문장을 의문문으로 바꿔 쓰세요.

1. The dog played with a ball. → _____

2. Grandpa sat on the bench. → _____

3. The horse ran a race. → _____

4. It snowed yesterday. → _____

C 그림을 보고 빈칸에 알맞은 단어를 골라 넣어 대화를 완성하세요.

did   make   no   finish   did   didn't   yes   he

1.

A: Did you see stars?

B. _____, I _____. It was cloudy.

2.

A: Did Anna _____ her homework?

B: Yes, she _____.

3.

A: _____ he go to the zoo?

B: No, _____ didn't. He felt sick.

4.

A: Did they _____ a snowman?

B: _____, they did.

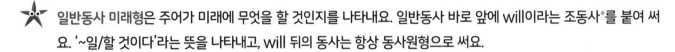

★ 일반동사 미래형은 주어가 미래에 무엇을 할 것인지를 나타내요. 일반동사 바로 앞에 will이라는 조동사*를 붙여 써요. '~일/할 것이다'라는 뜻을 나타내고, will 뒤의 동사는 항상 동사원형으로 써요.

I will visit America. 나는 미국에 방문할 거야.　　　You will love it. 너는 그것을 좋아할 거야.

*조동사는 동사를 도와주는 역할을 해요. 조동사에 대한 자세한 설명은 p.109를 참고하세요.

★ 일반동사 미래형의 부정문은 주어가 미래에 무엇을 하지 않을 것인지를 나타내는 문장이에요. 조동사 will 다음에 not을 쓰면 되며, '~하지 않을 것이다'라는 뜻을 나타내요.

She will not eat the pizza. 그녀는 피자를 먹지 않을 거야.

They will not play the game. 그들은 그 게임을 하지 않을 거야.

 will not은 won't로 줄여 쓸 수 있어요.　　We <u>won't</u> be late. 우리는 늦지 않을 거야.

★ 일반동사 미래형의 의문문은 주어가 미래에 무엇을 할 것인지, 또는 어떠할지를 묻는 문장이에요. Will을 문장 맨 앞으로 보내고 문장 끝에 물음표를 붙여요.

Will you come to my house? 너 우리집에 올래?　⇒　Yes, I will. / No, I won't.

Will it rain today? 오늘 비가 올까?　　　　　⇒　Yes, it will. / No, it won't.

★ will이 아직 확정되지 않은 미래의 일이나 계획에 대해 말한다면, be going to는 이미 확정된 미래의 일을 나타낼 때 사용해요. be동사는 주어에 맞게 am, are, is를 사용하면 돼요.

I am going to buy a new book. 나는 새 책 한 권을 살 거야.

We are going to meet your teacher. 우리는 너희 선생님을 뵐 거야.

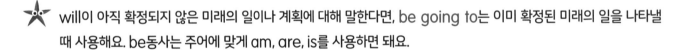 차곡차곡 기초 다지기

다음 중 올바른 문장에 V표 하세요.

1. I will writing a letter. ☐　　　I will write a letter. ☐
2. Will Steve make lunch? ☐　　　Will Steve makes lunch? ☐
3. Tom not will run. ☐　　　　　Tom will not run. ☐
4. We is going to play. ☐　　　　We are going to play. ☐

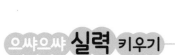

으쌰으쌰 **실력** 키우기

Ⓐ 다음 중 알맞은 것에 동그라미 하세요.

1. I will not no watch a movie.

2. Carol is going to swims swim .

3. Are Will you study science?

4. My sister will plays play the violin.

Ⓑ 다음 긍정문을 괄호 안의 형태에 맞게 바꿔 쓰세요.

1. We will exercise. → _____ (부정문)

2. Loren will return the book. → _____ (의문문)

3. I will finish my work. → _____ (부정문)

4. Grandmother will visit us. → _____ (의문문)

Ⓒ 그림을 보고 빈칸에 알맞은 단어를 골라 넣어 대화를 완성하세요.

| yes | no | I | play | will | go | help | won't |

1.

A: _____ you fly a kite?

B: Yes, _____ will.

2.

A: Will she _____ to the beach?

B: No, she _____ . She will go to the mountain.

3.

A: Will you _____ me?

B: _____, I will.

4.

A: Will they _____ tennis?

B: _____, they won't. They will swim.

1. 다음 중 현재진행형의 쓰임이 바른 문장을 고르세요.

① Is Brad clean the room?
② I am brushing my hair.
③ The lion is no sleeping.
④ They is not singing.
⑤ Is you working?

2. 다음 중 be동사 과거형의 쓰임이 바른 문장을 고르세요.

① They were be in Pohang.
② I were a baby.
③ She is was a student.
④ We was at the library.
⑤ Were you scared?

3. 다음 중 일반동사 과거형의 쓰임이 바른 문장을 고르세요.

① They was listened to the radio.
② Janice studied English.
③ Susan was remember my name.
④ The officer wrote a note.
⑤ The beavers wents into the river.

4. 다음 중 미래형의 쓰임이 바른 문장을 고르세요.

① I will am happy.
② She will not goes to the playground.
③ They will live in Hawaii.
④ Susan will sings a song.
⑤ The children will not visited museum.

[5~10] 단어를 바르게 배열하여 문장을 완성하세요.

5. a card   Noah   writing   is

➡ _____

6. Will   go to   you   the park

➡ _____

7. were   hot   They

➡ _____

8. didn't   the book   We   read

➡ _____

9. on the sofa   She   slept

➡ _____

10. is going to   It   rain

➡ _____

[11~14] 다음 보기 중 질문에 알맞은 대답을 고르세요.

① Yes, it was.   ② No, she didn't.
③ Yes, he will.   ④ No, they aren't.

11. A: Are they swimming?
B: (   )

12. A: Did she draw a picture?
B: (   )

13. A: Will he fix the car?
    B: (   )

14. A: Was the dog sick?
    B: (   )

[15~19] 다음 문장에서 틀린 부분을 찾아 바르게 고쳐 쓰세요.

15. We are jump on the bed.
    우리는 침대 위에서 뛰고 있다.

    ➡ _____

16. The girl didn't closed the door.
    그 소녀는 문을 닫지 않았다.

    ➡ _____

17. The children was not hungry.
    그 아이들은 배고프지 않았다.

    ➡ _____

18. We will promised you.
    우리가 너에게 약속할게.

    ➡ _____

19. He is works at the office.
    그는 사무실에서 일하고 있다.

    ➡ _____

[20~21] 그림을 보고 알맞은 것에 동그라미 하세요.

20.

    A: Is Are you skating?
    B: Yes No , we are.
       We're have having fun.

21.

    A: Did Tom ride rides a bike?
    B: No, he did didn't .
       He play played basketball.

[22~25] 빈칸에 알맞은 단어를 골라 넣어 글을 완성하세요.

didn't	met	go	were

Jenny [22] _____ Susie. They [23] _____ at the beach. They [24] _____ swim. They made a sandcastle. They had a fun time. They will [25] _____ to the beach again one day

Chapter 07

형용사와 부사

Joy 쌤

Minho, you are smart.

Minho

갑자기 제 칭찬을…

Joy 쌤

여기서 smart가 바로 형용사야. '똑똑한'이라는 성질을 나타내지.

Minho

앗, 전 또 제 칭찬하시는 줄…

Joy 쌤

Yes, you are very smart.

Minho

네? 헤헷. 감사해요.

Joy 쌤

여기서 very처럼 다른 형용사를 꾸며주면서 문장을
더 자세하게 설명해주는 단어를 부사라고 해.

Minho

Joy 쌤

민호가 똑똑한 건 사실이고!^^ 그럼 형용사와 부사를
사용해서 문장을 꾸미는 방법을 알려줄게.

Unit 1 형용사의 의미와 쓰임

⭐ 형용사는 명사의 모양이나 크기, 상태, 색깔, 수 등을 자세하게 설명하는 역할을 해요.

모양, 크기	round, square, straight, flat, long, tall, short, big, small
상태	hot, cold, warm, cool, happy, sad, tired, sleepy, pretty, old
색깔	red, orange, yellow, green, blue, purple, black, white, silver, gold
수	one, two, three, four, five, six, seven, eight, nine, ten

⭐ 형용사가 명사를 꾸며 설명하는 방법은 두 가지가 있어요.

1. 명사 앞에서 명사를 꾸며요.

John has a <u>blue</u> <u>backpack</u>. 존은 파란 가방을 가지고 있어.

<u>Beautiful</u> <u>flowers</u> smell good. 아름다운 꽃들은 향기가 좋아.

2. be동사 뒤에서 문장의 주어를 자세히 설명해요.

<u>Her dress</u> is <u>long</u>. 그녀의 드레스는 길어. (Her dress가 long)

<u>The children</u> are <u>happy</u>. 그 아이들은 행복해. (The children이 happy)

 차곡차곡 기초 다지기

다음 중 형용사가 아닌 것을 찾아 동그라미 하세요.

1. sad   easy   car

2. nice   weather   tall

3. game   sweet   good

4. fast   short   candy

5. pretty   test   new

6. book   kind   warm

7. small   eye   hungry

8. happy   strong   apple

으쌰으쌰 실력 키우기

Ⓐ 빈칸에 알맞은 형용사를 골라 넣어 문장을 완성하세요.

old   red   ten   big   slow

1. It is a _____ bicycle. 그것은 빨간 자전거이다.

2. Snails are _____ . 달팽이들은 느리다.

3. The dog is _____ . 그 개는 크다.

4. They have an _____ house. 그들은 오래된 집을 가지고 있다.

5. Jen has _____ roses. 젠은 열 송이 장미를 가지고 있다.

Ⓑ 다음 문장에서 형용사를 찾아 동그라미 한 후, 형용사가 꾸미는 명사에 밑줄 치세요.

1. She has a round face.

2. It is a lovely picture.

3. The rabbit is soft.

4. The teacher is kind.

5. David is brave.

6. He has short hair.

Ⓒ 그림을 보고 빈칸에 알맞은 형용사를 골라 넣어 글을 완성하세요.

1.

I'm a giraffe.

1) I live in _____ Africa.

2) I'm _____ .

3) I have a _____ neck.

tall
long
hot

2.

I'm a shark.

1) I live in the _____ sea.

2) I'm a _____ swimmer.

3) I have _____ teeth.

sharp
deep
fast

Unit 2 수량형용사

수량형용사는 명사의 수와 양이 많고 적음을 나타내며, <수량형용사 + 명사> 형태로 쓰여요.

1. many와 much는 둘 다 '많은'이라는 뜻이지만, 뒤에 오는 명사가 달라요.

many (수가) 많은	many + 복수 명사	I have many books. 나는 많은 책을 가지고 있어.
much (양이) 많은	much + 셀 수 없는 명사	Ella didn't eat much food. 엘라는 음식을 많이 먹지 않았어.

2. every와 all은 둘 다 '모든'이라는 뜻이지만, every 뒤에는 단수 명사, all 뒤에는 복수 명사가 와요.

every (각각의) 모든	every + 단수 명사	Every student has a backpack. 모든 학생은 책가방을 가지고 있어.
all (전체의) 모든	all + 복수 명사	All tickets are expensive. 모든 티켓이 비싸.

3. some과 any는 '약간의'라는 뜻으로, some은 긍정문, any는 부정문이나 의문문에서 쓰여요.

some (긍정문) 약간의	some + 복수 명사/셀 수 없는 명사	There are some flowers in the vase. 꽃병에 약간의 꽃이 있어. I have some money. 나는 돈이 약간 있어.
any (부정문) 조금도 (의문문) 약간의	any + 복수 명사/셀 수 없는 명사	They didn't have any questions. 그들은 어떠한 질문도 없었어. Do you have any time? 시간이 좀 있니?

> **Tip** 권유나 부탁을 나타낼 때는 some이 의문문에 쓰이기도 해요.
> Do you want <u>some</u> tea? 차 좀 마실래?   Can I eat <u>some</u> cookies? 쿠키 좀 먹어도 되나요?

차곡차곡 기초 다지기

<수량형용사 + 명사> 형태가 바르면 ○에, 틀리면 ✕에 V표 하세요.

1. much times 많은 시간　○ □　✕ □
2. every chair 모든 의자　○ □　✕ □
3. some bread 약간의 빵　○ □　✕ □
4. many money 많은 돈　○ □　✕ □
5. all trees 모든 나무들　○ □　✕ □
6. much water 많은 물　○ □　✕ □
7. many friends 많은 친구들　○ □　✕ □
8. every cars 모든 자동차　○ □　✕ □

A many와 much 중 알맞은 것에 동그라미 하세요.

1. Many Much animals live in the jungle.

2. I don't have many much time.

3. Kate didn't drink many much milk.

4. Many Much children played at the pool.

B 빈칸에 every와 all 중 알맞은 것을 쓰세요.

1. _____ elephants have big ears.

2. The teacher sent an email to _____ students.

3. Mike played _____ soccer game.

4. We study English _____ morning.

C 그림을 보고 빈칸에 some과 any 중 알맞은 것을 넣어 대화를 완성하세요.

1.

A: Do you want _____ water?

B: Yes, please. I'm thirsty.

2.

A: Are you busy?

B: Yes, I am. I don't have _____ time.

3.

A: What did you eat?

B: I ate _____ sandwiches.

4.

A: Do you have _____ pens?

B: No, I don't. Sorry.

Unit 3 부사의 의미와 쓰임

⭐ 부사는 형용사나 동사, 다른 부사를 꾸며주면서 그 의미를 더 자세하게 나타내는 단어예요.

형용사를 꾸밀 때	Air is very important. 공기는 매우 중요해요.
동사를 꾸밀 때	The teacher speaks softly. 그 선생님은 부드럽게 말씀하셔.
다른 부사를 꾸밀 때	Bob walks very quickly. 밥은 매우 빨리 걸어.

⭐ 일반적으로 부사는 형용사에 -ly를 붙여서 만들어요.

대부분의 형용사	+ -ly	real 진짜의 ➡ really 정말로　　soft 부드러운 ➡ softly 부드럽게 clear 명확한 ➡ clearly 분명히　　slow 느린 ➡ slowly 천천히 sad 슬픈 ➡ sadly 슬프게　　careful 조심하는 ➡ carefully 조심스럽게
y로 끝나는 형용사	y ➡ i + -ly	happy 행복한 ➡ happily 행복하게　　easy 쉬운 ➡ easily 쉽게 busy 바쁜 ➡ busily 바쁘게　　heavy 무거운 ➡ heavily 무겁게
형용사와 부사의 형태가 같은 경우		fast 빠른 ➡ fast 빠르게　　high 높은 ➡ high 높이 late 늦은 ➡ late 늦게　　early 이른 ➡ early 일찍 bright 밝은 ➡ bright 밝게　　hard 열심히 하는 ➡ hard 열심히

⭐ 그 외에 자주 쓰이는 부사들도 알아 두세요.

very 매우, 아주　　well 잘　　soon 곧　　so 너무　　too 너무　　now 지금　　alone 혼자

They finished it so well. 그들은 그것을 아주 잘 마쳤어.
The train will arrive soon. 그 기차는 곧 도착할 거야.

차곡차곡 기초 다지기

다음 중 부사를 모두 찾아 동그라미 하세요.

cat	bread	really	early	morning
sun	very	juice	happily	family
softly	box	read	carefully	fly
make	now	watch	book	clearly

 실력 키우기

A 다음 문장에서 부사를 찾아 동그라미 하세요.

1. The pizza is really big.　　　　　2. She cried sadly.

3. The turtle moves slowly.　　　　4. Beth read the letter carefully.

5. The weather is so nice.　　　　　6. My mom gets up early.

B 밑줄 친 부사가 꾸미는 형용사, 동사, 혹은 다른 부사를 찾아 화살표로 연결하세요.

1. The little duck is <u>so</u> cute.　　　2. Ellen did her work <u>well</u>.

3. The girls answered <u>politely</u>.　　　4. My teacher talks <u>too</u> fast.

5. I finished the homework <u>finally</u>.　6. It is <u>very</u> cold in Alaska.

C 빈칸에 알맞은 단어를 골라 넣어 문장을 완성하세요.

hard　　　happily　　　really　　　now　　　bright　　　too

1. The sun shines _____. 해가 밝게 빛난다.

2. This is _____ delicious 이거 진짜 맛있다.

3. The man is _____ busy. 그 남자는 너무 바쁘다.

4. The baby is sleeping _____. 그 아기는 지금 자고 있다.

5. They smiled _____. 그들은 행복하게 미소지었다.

6. We studied _____ for the test. 우리는 그 시험을 위해 열심히 공부했다.

Unit 4 빈도부사

⭐ 빈도부사는 주어가 어떤 일을 얼마나 자주 하는지 알려주는 부사예요.

| 0% | ←————————————→ | 100% |

never	rarely	sometimes	often	usually	always
전혀	드물게	가끔	자주	보통	항상

⭐ 문장에서 빈도부사의 위치는 동사에 따라 달라져요.

1. be동사 + 빈도부사

Larry is usually active. 래리는 보통 활동적이야.

The restaurant is often busy. 그 식당은 자주 붐벼.

2. 빈도부사 + 일반동사

They sometimes make gimbap. 그들은 가끔 김밥을 만들어.

I rarely drink milk in the morning. 나는 아침에 우유를 거의 마시지 않아.

He never eats cucumbers. 그는 절대 오이를 먹지 않아.

> **Tip** 부정의 의미를 갖는 never는 '절대/전혀 ~하지 않는다', rarely는 '좀처럼 ~하지 않는다'라는 뜻으로 쓰여요.

3. 조동사 + 빈도부사 + 일반동사

I will always love you. 나는 너를 항상 사랑할 거야.

The students can usually speak two languages. 그 학생들은 보통 두 가지 언어를 말할 수 있어요.

차곡차곡 기초 다지기

알맞은 단어를 써서 퍼즐을 완성하세요.

가로

1. 보통
2. 가끔
3. 전혀

세로

4. 드물게
5. 항상
6. 자주

으쌰으쌰 실력 키우기

Ⓐ 다음 문장에서 빈도부사를 찾아 동그라미 하세요.

1. Kevin never drinks milk.
2. I often go to school early.
3. We are always happy.
4. Bob is usually shy.
5. My family rarely eats outside.
6. My dog sometimes takes a nap.

Ⓑ 괄호 안의 빈도부사를 넣어 문장을 다시 쓰세요.

1. Becky watches a movie. (sometimes) ➡ _____

2. My parents are patient. (always) ➡ _____

3. I finish my homework. (usually) ➡ _____

4. He will buy toys. (never) ➡ _____

5. It snows in Texas. (rarely) ➡ _____

6. He is late for school. (often) ➡ _____

Ⓒ 단어를 바르게 배열하여 문장을 완성하세요.

1. he / always / nice / is ➡ _____
그는 언제나 친절하다.

2. often / reads books / she ➡ _____
그녀는 자주 책을 읽는다.

3. will / you / never / I / forget ➡ _____
나는 너를 절대 잊지 않을 거야.

4. sometimes / they / play tennis ➡ _____
그들은 가끔 테니스를 친다.

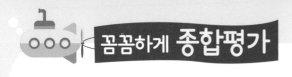

꼼꼼하게 종합평가

1. 다음 중 형용사를 모두 고르세요.
   ① he   ② dirty
   ③ run   ④ big
   ⑤ computer

2. 다음 중 수량 형용사가 <u>아닌</u> 것을 고르세요.
   ① many   ② some
   ③ every   ④ much
   ⑤ always

3. 다음 중 부사를 고르세요.
   ① teacher   ② very
   ③ have   ④ kind
   ⑤ box

4. 다음 중 빈도부사가 <u>아닌</u> 것을 고르세요.
   ① usually   ② never
   ③ any   ④ sometimes
   ⑤ often

5. 다음 중 형용사의 쓰임이 바른 문장을 고르세요.
   ① Look at the flower beautiful.
   ② I am fast.
   ③ They have balls three.
   ④ He slow is.
   ⑤ Susan kind is.

6. 다음 중 수량 형용사의 쓰임이 바른 문장을 고르세요.
   ① He doesn't have many time.
   ② All cake is delicious.
   ③ Every children has a dream.
   ④ We have many friends.
   ⑤ I have books some.

7. 다음 중 부사가 쓰이지 <u>않은</u> 문장을 고르세요.
   ① The boy sings happily.
   ② The students are studying at the library.
   ③ The weather is so nice.
   ④ He came late.
   ⑤ The movie is very interesting.

8. 다음 중 빈도부사가 <u>잘못</u> 쓰인 문장을 고르세요.
   ① He usually goes to bed early.
   ② They are never bad.
   ③ I will always remember you.
   ④ She often plays soccer.
   ⑤ My cat sometimes is lazy.

[9~12] 단어를 바르게 배열하여 문장을 완성하세요.

9. | huge | The elephant | is |

   ➡ _____

10. | don't | any | have | milk | I |

   ➡ _____

11. | are | You | wonderful | really |

   ➡ _____

12. | English | always | study | We |

   ➡ _____

[13~16] 빈칸에 알맞은 말을 고르세요.

13. _____ fruits are fresh.
① Much   ② Usually   ③ All
④ Any   ⑤ Every

14. The bird flies very _____.
① small   ② happy   ③ many
④ high   ⑤ sometimes

15. Wilson _____ plays basketball.
① well   ② often   ③ every
④ some   ⑤ many

16. I am _____ cold now.
① all   ② many   ③ so
④ any   ⑤ much

[17~19] 다음 문장에서 **틀린** 부분을 찾아 바르게 고쳐 쓰세요.

17. My uncle has hair brown.

➡ _____

18. I exercise every days.

➡ _____

19. The woman buys often fresh eggs.

➡ _____

[20~21] 그림을 보고 알맞은 것에 동그라미 하세요.

20.

A: This soup is ⬚all too⬚ hot.
B: Yes. But it's ⬚really many⬚ delicious, too.

21.

A: Do you have ⬚any much⬚ questions?
B: Yes. I have ⬚every some⬚ questions.

[22~25] 빈칸에 알맞은 단어를 골라 넣어 글을 완성하세요.

writes	very	alone	sometimes

Jenny is ²² _____ in her room. She ²³ _____ has quiet time. She usually ²⁴ _____ in a journal. She likes writing ²⁵ _____ much.

*journal 일기

Chapter 08

비교급과 전치사

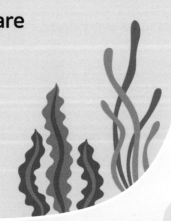

Joy 쌤

Hi, Minho. 슈퍼맨이랑 헐크 중에 누가 더 힘이 셀까?

Minho

Good morning, Ms. Joy.
슈퍼맨도 힘이 세지만 헐크가 힘이 더 셀 것 같아요.

Joy 쌤

'헐크가 슈퍼맨보다 힘이 더 세다.'
이렇게 비교하는 문장을 비교급이라고 해.

Minho

선생님, 그런데 아이언맨이 가장 힘이 센 것 같아요.

Joy 쌤

'아이언맨이 슈퍼히어로 중에 가장 힘이 세다.'
이 문장은 최상급이야.

Minho

아무래도 비교급과 최상급을 배울 차례인가 봐요?

Joy 쌤

맞아. 그리고 시간, 장소, 방향을 나타내는
전치사도 함께 배워보자. Let's get started!

Unit 1 비교급

⭐ 비교급은 두 사람이나 두 개의 사물을 비교할 때 사용해요. 비교급은 형용사에 -er을 붙여 만들고, '더 ~한'이라는 뜻이에요. 비교 대상 앞에 than을 써서 '~보다'라는 뜻을 나타내요.

비교급 + than + 비교 대상: ~보다 더 …한

I am tall.
나는 키가 커.

I am taller than you.
나는 너보다 키가 더 커.

1음절 단어	+ -er	short ➡ shorter 더 키가 작은 young ➡ younger 더 어린
e로 끝나는 단어	+ -r	nice ➡ nicer 더 좋은 large ➡ larger 더 큰
'자음 + 모음 + 자음'의 1음절 단어	+ 마지막 자음 + -er	hot ➡ hotter 더 뜨거운 big ➡ bigger 더 큰
y로 끝나는 2음절 단어	y ➡ i + -er	happy ➡ happier 더 행복한 busy ➡ busier 더 바쁜
2음절 이상의 단어	more + 형용사	beautiful ➡ more beautiful 더 아름다운 delicious ➡ more delicious 더 맛있는
불규칙적으로 변하는 형용사		good ➡ better 더 좋은 bad ➡ worse 더 나쁜

He is smarter than me. 그는 나보다 더 똑똑해.

They are more famous than us. 그들은 우리보다 더 유명해.

Today is better than yesterday. 오늘이 어제보다 더 좋아.

차곡차곡 **기초** 다지기

다음 중 비교급을 찾아 동그라미 하세요.

1. teacher   good   colder

2. shorter   dancer   lazy

3. fast   hotter   baker

4. hard   softer   driver

5. manager   sour   prettier

6. writer   fun   larger

 **실력** 키우기

Ⓐ 다음 형용사를 비교급으로 바꿔 쓰세요.

1. clean → _____

2. bad → _____

3. long → _____

4. exciting → _____

5. heavy → _____

6. difficult → _____

7. nice → _____

8. big → _____

Ⓑ 괄호 안의 단어를 사용해 비교급 문장을 완성하세요.

1. Andy is _____ than Tom. (young)

2. My father is _____ than us. (wise)

3. Love is _____ _____ than hate. (powerful)

4. Honey is _____ than candy. (sweet)

5. Potatoes are _____ than onions. (cheap)

6. A turtle is _____ than a rabbit. (slow)

Ⓒ 다음 문장에서 <u>틀린</u> 부분을 찾아 바르게 고쳐 쓰세요.

1. She is more busy than me. → _____

2. A giraffe is tall than an elephant. → _____

3. I am than faster you. → _____

4. Apples are biger than cherries. → _____

5. English is interestinger than math. → _____

Unit 2 최상급

⭐ 최상급은 셋 이상의 대상을 비교하여 정도가 가장 높음을 나타내요. 최상급은 형용사에 -est를 붙여 만들고, '가장 ~한'이라는 뜻이에요. 최상급 앞에는 the를 붙여요.

> **the + 최상급 + in + 전체 비교 그룹: ~ 중에서 가장 …한**

I am the tallest in the jungle.
나는 정글에서 가장 키가 커.

⭐ 형용사의 음절에 따라 최상급을 만드는 규칙이 있어요.

1음절 단어	+ -est	short ➡ shortest 가장 키가 작은 young ➡ youngest 가장 어린
e로 끝나는 단어	+ -st	nice ➡ nicest 가장 좋은 large ➡ largest 가장 큰
'자음 + 모음 + 자음'의 1음절 단어	+ 마지막 자음 + -est	hot ➡ hottest 가장 뜨거운 big ➡ biggest 가장 큰
y로 끝나는 2음절 단어	y ➡ i + -est	happy ➡ happiest 가장 행복한 busy ➡ busiest 가장 바쁜
2음절 이상의 단어	most + 형용사	beautiful ➡ most beautiful 가장 아름다운 delicious ➡ most delicious 가장 맛있는
불규칙적으로 변하는 형용사		good ➡ best 가장 좋은 bad ➡ worst 가장 나쁜

She is the youngest in her family. 그녀는 그녀의 가족 중에서 가장 어려.

You are the happiest child in the world. 너는 세상에서 가장 행복한 어린이야.

They are the best team in the class. 그들은 그 반에서 최고의 팀이야.

차곡차곡 기초 다지기

다음 중 최상급을 모두 찾아 동그라미 하세요.

nest	best	higher	cuter
west	coldest	faster	largest
rest	vest	more	worst
test	biggest	east	easiest

으쌰으쌰 **실력** 키우기

Ⓐ 다음 형용사를 최상급으로 바꿔 쓰세요.

1. sweet → _____   2. long → _____

3. busy → _____   4. hot → _____

5. thick → _____   6. difficult → _____

7. happy → _____   8. important → _____

Ⓑ 괄호 안의 단어를 사용해 최상급 문장을 완성하세요.

1.

The elephant is _____ _____ animal in the jungle. (large)

2.

Mount Everest is _____ _____ mountain in the world. (high)

3.

It is _____ _____ _____ road in the city. (dangerous)

4.
Football is _____ _____ _____ sport in America. (popular)

Ⓒ 단어를 바르게 배열하여 문장을 완성하세요.

1. in the sky / the biggest / star / it / is   그것은 하늘에서 가장 큰 별이다.

   → _____

2. am / in my class / I / the fastest   나는 우리 반에서 가장 빠르다.

   → _____

3. is / the most beautiful / it / day / in my life   내 인생에서 가장 아름다운 날이다.

   → _____

Unit 3 시간 전치사

⭐ 전치사는 명사 앞에 쓰여 시간, 장소, 방향 등을 나타내는 단어예요. 시간이나 때를 나타내는 명사 앞에 쓰는 다양한 시간 전치사가 있어요.

in ～에	연도, 달, 계절, 하루의 특정한 때	in 2018 2018년에 in spring 봄에	in July 7월에 in the morning 아침에
on ～에	정확한 날짜, 요일, 공휴일	on May 11th 5월 11일에 on Christmas Day 크리스마스에	on Sunday 일요일에
at ～에	정확한 시간, 하루의 특정한 때	at 6 o'clock 6시에	at night 밤에
after ～ 후에	시간, 때, 요일	after 9 o'clock 9시 이후에 after Friday 금요일 이후에	after school 방과 후에
before ～ 전에	시간, 때, 요일	before 4:30 4시 30분 이전에 before Saturday 토요일 전에	before dinner 저녁 식사 전에

I was born in 2002. 나는 2002년에 태어났어.

Flowers bloom in spring. 꽃들은 봄에 피어.

My birthday is on May 11th. 내 생일은 5월 11일이야.

We will go on a picnic on Sunday. 우리는 일요일에 소풍을 갈 거야.

Let's meet at 6 o'clock. 6시에 만나자.

I go to bed after 9 o'clock. 나는 9시 이후에 자러 가.

I will finish my homework before Saturday. 나는 토요일 전에 숙제를 끝낼 거야.

 for와 during은 '～ 동안'이라는 뜻이에요. for 뒤에는 숫자로 나타내는 시간을 쓰고, during 뒤에는 행사나 사건을 나타내는 시간을 써요.

Mom cooked dinner <u>for two hours</u>. 엄마가 두 시간 동안 저녁 식사를 요리했어.

We had fun <u>during summer vacation</u>. 우리는 여름 방학 동안 재미있게 지냈어.

차곡차곡 기초 다지기

빈칸에 알맞은 전치사를 쓰세요.

1. _____ winter 겨울에

2. _____ Wednesday 수요일 이후에

3. _____ lunch 점심 식사 전에

4. _____ August 17th 8월 17일에

5. _____ 2010 2010년에

6. _____ 7 o'clock 7시에

으쌰으쌰 실력 키우기

Ⓐ 다음 시간 표현에 알맞은 전치사에 동그라미 하세요.

1. in on at 1912
2. in on at Monday

3. in on at New Year's Day
4. in on at 3 o'clock

5. in on at January 5th
6. in on at summer

Ⓑ 빈칸에 알맞은 전치사를 골라 넣어 문장을 완성하세요.

on   at   before   in   after

1. The train comes _____ 6:30. 그 기차는 6시 30분에 온다.

2. My mom's birthday is _____ winter. 우리 엄마의 생신은 겨울에 있다.

3. Daniel reads books _____ breakfast. 대니얼은 아침 식사 후에 책을 읽는다.

4. Children are celebrated _____ Children's Day. 어린이들은 어린이날에 축하받는다.

5. I will come back _____ 4 o'clock. 저는 4시 전에 돌아올게요.

Ⓒ 빈칸에 알맞은 전치사를 써서 문장을 완성하세요.

1. I traveled to Paris _____ 10 days. 나는 10일 동안 파리를 여행했다.

2. Please wash your hands _____ dinner. 저녁 식사 전에 손을 씻으세요.

3. The restaurant is closed _____ Sunday. 그 식당은 일요일에 문을 닫는다.

4. I am going to London _____ November. 나는 11월에 런던에 갈 예정이다.

5. We will go to the park _____ school. 우리는 방과 후에 공원에 갈 것이다.

6. My summer vacation starts _____ July 27th. 내 여름 방학은 7월 27일에 시작한다.

Unit 4 장소/방향 전치사

⭐ 장소나 방향을 나타내는 다양한 전치사가 있어요.

in	~ 안에	in the bag 가방 안에 in Korea 한국에
on	~ 위에	on the bed 침대 위에 on the desk 책상 위에
under	~ 아래에	under the chair 의자 아래에 under the sea 바다 밑에
next to	~ 옆에	next to the book 책 옆에 next to the library 도서관 옆에
in front of	~ 앞에	in front of me 내 앞에 in front of the store 가게 앞에
behind	~ 뒤에	behind the door 문 뒤에 behind the stage 무대 뒤에
from	~부터, ~에서(출신)	from here 여기서부터 from Seoul 서울에서
to	~로, ~에게	to Beijing 베이징으로 to you 너에게

I have some pens in the bag. 나는 가방 안에 펜 몇 개를 가지고 있어.

A pillow is on the bed. 베개가 침대 위에 있어.

She found an eraser under the chair. 그녀는 의자 밑에서 지우개를 찾았어.

Tom is standing next to Jane. 톰이 제인 옆에 서 있어.

There is a car in front of my house. 우리집 앞에 차 한 대가 있어.

Many people work behind the stage. 많은 사람들이 무대 뒤에서 일해.

We are from Seoul. 우리는 서울 출신이야.

They will fly to Beijing. 그들은 베이징으로 비행기를 타고 갈 거야.

> **Tip** 비교적 넓은 장소 앞에는 in, 비교적 좁은 장소 앞에는 at을 써요.
> I live <u>in</u> Korea. 나는 한국에 살아.   I am <u>at</u> home. 나는 집에 있어.

 차곡차곡 **기초** 다지기

알맞은 단어를 써서 퍼즐을 완성하세요.

가로

1. ~ 아래에

2. ~ 옆에

3. ~ 위에

4. ~ 앞에

세로

5. ~ 안에

6. ~ 뒤에

7. ~로, ~에게

8. ~로부터

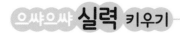

A 빈칸에 알맞은 전치사를 쓰세요.

1. _____ the desk 책상 밑에
2. _____ the classroom 교실 안에
3. _____ the door 문 뒤에
4. _____ the post office 우체국 옆에
5. _____ school 학교로
6. _____ the truck 트럭 앞에
7. _____ the chair 의자 위에
8. _____ Gyeongju 경주로부터

B 괄호 안의 전치사를 알맞은 자리에 써서 문장을 다시 쓰세요.

1. Your key is the table. (on)   → _____

2. Erin sits Doyoung. (next to)   → _____

3. The cat is hiding the box. (behind)   → _____

4. They are swimming the pool. (in)   → _____

C 그림을 보고 단어를 바르게 배열하여 문장을 완성하세요.

1.   from / Miles / South Africa / is
   → _____

2.  is / his house / in front of / a dog
   → _____

3.  the students / the library / walking / to / are
   → _____

4.  the vase / are / some flowers / in
   → _____

Unit 5 There is, There are

★ There is, There are는 '~(들)이 있다'라는 뜻으로, 전치사구*와 함께 잘 쓰여요.

There is + 단수 명사 + 전치사구: ～에 …이 있다

긍정문 There is **a book** on my desk. 내 책상 위에 책이 한 권 있어.

There is **some milk** in the fridge. 냉장고 안에 우유가 좀 있어.

부정문 There isn't **a boy** next to the tree. 나무 옆에 소년이 없어.

의문문 Is there **a cat** under the table? 탁자 아래에 고양이가 있나요?

Yes, there is. 네, 있어요. / No, there isn't. 아니요, 없어요.

*전치사구란 on the table(탁자 위에), in the box(상자 안에)처럼 〈전치사 + 명사〉 형태로 된 구를 말해요.

There are + 복수 명사 + 전치사구: ～에 …들이 있다

긍정문 There are **three people** in front of me. 내 앞에 세 사람이 있어.

부정문 There aren't **any houses** behind the beach. 해변가 뒤로는 어떠한 집도 없어.

의문문 Are there **any old pictures** from Germany? 독일에서 온 오래된 그림들이 있나요?

Yes, there are. 네, 있어요. / No, there aren't. 아니요, 없어요.

> **Tip** There is, There are의 과거는 There was, There were로 '~(들)이 있었다'라는 뜻이에요.
> <u>There was</u> a festival in Venice. 베네치아에서 축제가 있었어.
> <u>There were</u> two dogs on the street. 길 위에 개 두 마리가 있었어.

차곡차곡 **기초** 다지기

There is, There are 뒤에 올 수 있는 명사에 바르게 연결하세요.

shoes ·   · an ant

a pencil ·   ·   · ten apples

cherries ·   · some water

ducks ·   · ·   · many children

a book ·   · a slide

Ⓐ 다음 중 알맞은 것에 동그라미 하세요.

1. There is There are a toothbrush. 2. There is There are many visitors.

3. There is There are a house. 4. There is There are some apples.

Ⓑ 다음 긍정문을 괄호 안의 형태에 맞게 바꿔 쓰세요.

1. There is a bus to the museum.

　➡ _____ (부정문)

2. There are two children in front of the gate.

　➡ _____ (의문문)

3. There are butterflies on the flower.

　➡ _____ (부정문)

4. There is a candy in the drawer.

　➡ _____ (의문문)

Ⓒ 그림을 보고 질문에 알맞은 대답을 쓰세요.

1.

A: Is there a cup on the table?

B: _____, _____ _____.

2.

A: Are there pandas in the zoo?

B: ___, _____ _____.

3.

A: Is there a cat next to the girl?

B: _____, _____ _____.

4.

A: Are there many books in the library?

B: _____, _____ _____.

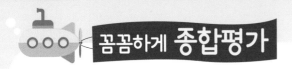

1. 다음 중 비교급이 <u>아닌</u> 것을 고르세요.
   ① taller ② sweeter
   ③ smaller ④ largest
   ⑤ more interesting

2. 다음 중 최상급이 <u>아닌</u> 것을 고르세요.
   ① biggest ② fastest
   ③ most active ④ coldest
   ⑤ fatter

3. 다음 중 전치사가 <u>잘못</u> 쓰인 문장을 고르세요.
   ① I was born in 2010.
   ② They will meet their friends on 6:00.
   ③ He goes to the park on Wednesday.
   ④ She eats lunch at 12:30.
   ⑤ The dog sleeps before 8 o'clock.

4. 다음 중 전치사의 쓰임이 바른 문장을 고르세요.
   ① Mom went to the post office.
   ② The girl is China from.
   ③ Billy is playing to next Cindy.
   ④ Your birthday present is the box in.
   ⑤ The apple is the under tree.

5. 다음 중 There is와 There are의 쓰임이 바르지 <u>않은</u> 문장을 고르세요.
   ① There are many cars in the parking lot.
   ② There are a notebook on the desk.
   ③ There isn't a ball under the table.
   ④ There is some ice cream in the fridge.
   ⑤ Is there a bus to the station?

[6~10] 빈칸에 알맞은 말을 고르세요.

6. My dog is _____ than your dog.
   ① smallest
   ② smaller
   ③ more small
   ④ small
   ⑤ the smallest

7. The bridge is the _____ in the world.
   ① short ② most short
   ③ shortest ④ shorter
   ⑤ shorter than

8. Many people swim _____ summer.
   ① on ② at ③ in
   ④ under ⑤ behind

9. The students are running _____ the playground.
   ① to ② during ③ under
   ④ after ⑤ before

10. _____ some rabbits in the garden.
    ① There is ② There are
    ③ It is ④ Are there
    ⑤ Is there

[11~15] 단어를 바르게 배열하여 문장을 완성하세요.

11. | are | on the tray | bananas | There |

    ➔ _____

12. waiting | are | behind the gate | They

➡ _____

13. English class | We | on Monday | have

➡ _____

14. the prettiest | in town | girl | She | is

➡ _____

15. A ship | a boat | bigger | is | than

➡ _____

[16~21] 다음 문장에서 <u>틀린</u> 부분을 찾아 바르게 고쳐 쓰세요.

16. Hope is more stronger than fear.
희망은 두려움보다 더 강하다.

➡ _____

17. My mother is the beautifulest woman in the world.
나의 어머니는 세상에서 가장 아름다운 여성이다.

➡ _____

18. We eat rice cake soup in New Year's Day.
우리는 설날에 떡국을 먹는다.

➡ _____

19. Is there a store behind the school?
학교 옆에 상점이 있나요?

➡ _____

20. The trip starts before July 23rd.
그 여행은 7월 23일에 시작된다.

➡ _____

21. There aren't any bread in the bakery.
빵집에 빵이 하나도 없다.

➡ _____

[22~25] 빈칸에 알맞은 단어를 골라 넣어 글을 완성하세요.

on   to   in   most

Jenny went ²² _____ America. There is a bridge ²³ _____ San Francisco. It is the ²⁴ _____ famous bridge in America. She took a picture ²⁵ _____ the bridge.

Chapter 09

조동사

Joy 쌤

Hello, Minho. 조동사가 뭔지 아니?

Minho

음… 동사랑 관련이 있는 것 같은데 잘 모르겠어요.

Joy 쌤

맞아. 조동사의 '조'는 '도울 조(助)' 자로, 동사를 도와준다는 뜻이야.

우리가 앞에서 3인칭 단수형을 만들 때 사용한 do나
미래형을 만들 때 사용한 will도 모두 조동사야.
동사와 함께 쓰여서 특정한 의미를 보태주는 역할을 하지.

이번 챕터에서는 새로운 조동사를 알려줄게.
can, may, must, should는 꼭 알아야 하는 조동사야.
I can play the piano.
I may play the piano.
I must play the piano.
I should play the piano.
조동사에 따라 문장의 뜻도 완전히 달라져.

Minho

문장의 뜻이 어떻게 달라지는지 자세히 알고 싶어요.

Joy 쌤

좋은 자세야! 그럼 시작해볼까?

Unit 1 can

⭐ 조동사는 동사를 도와 그 의미를 보태주는 역할을 하며, 주어와 상관없이 같은 형태를 써요. 조동사는 혼자 쓰일 수 없고, 항상 동사원형과 함께 쓰여요. can은 '~할 수 있다'라는 뜻을 가진 조동사로 동사원형 앞에 써요.

주어 + can + 동사원형

I can speak English. 나는 영어를 말할 수 있어.   We can make robots. 우리는 로봇을 만들 수 있어.

⭐ 조동사 can의 부정문은 cannot 혹은 can't를 동사원형 앞에 쓰며, '~할 수 없다'라는 뜻을 나타내요.

주어 + cannot(= can't) + 동사원형

You can not fix the car. 너는 그 차를 고칠 수 없어.   He can't swim well. 그는 수영을 잘하지 못해.

⭐ 조동사 can의 의문문은 can으로 문장을 시작하며, '~할 수 있니?'라는 뜻을 나타내요. 질문에 대한 대답은 <Yes, 주어 + can.>이나 <No, 주어 + can't.>로 써요.

Can + 주어 + 동사원형 ~?

Can you read Chinese? ➡ Yes, I can. 응, 할 수 있어. / No, I can't. 아니, 할 수 없어.
너는 중국어를 읽을 수 있니?

Can Jisung play soccer? ➡ Yes, he can. 응, 할 수 있어. / No, he can't. 아니, 할 수 없어.
지성이는 축구를 할 수 있니?

Tip Can I ~?에는 허락을 묻는 뜻이 있고, Can you ~?는 요청을 할 때 쓰이기도 해요.
Can I play outside? 저 밖에서 놀아도 되나요?
Can you open the window, please? 창문을 열어줄 수 있어요?

차곡차곡 기초 다지기

조동사 can 뒤에 오는 알맞은 형태에 동그라미 하세요.

1. can   write | writes   2. can   jump | jumped   3. can   sees | see

4. can   went | go   5. can   finish | finished   6. can   ate | eat

7. can   drinks | drink   8. can   speak | spoke   9. can   moves | move

A 조동사 can을 알맞은 자리에 넣어 문장을 다시 쓰세요.

1. They play tennis. ➡ _____

2. Spencer sings songs. ➡ _____

3. Lewis writes stories. ➡ _____

4. I climb the mountain. ➡ _____

B 다음 긍정문을 괄호 안의 형태에 맞게 바꿔 쓰세요.

1. We can watch the cartoon. ➡ _____ (의문문)

2. Ethan can drive a car. ➡ _____ (부정문)

3. You can clean your room. ➡ _____ (의문문)

4. Denise can ride a horse. ➡ _____ (부정문)

C 그림을 보고 빈칸에 알맞은 단어를 써서 대화를 완성하세요.

1.
A: _____ you speak French?
B: _____, _____ can. Bonjour!

2.
A: Can I go to the park?
B: No, _____ _____ .

3.
A: Can Tom cook?
B: Yes, _____ _____ . He is a good cook.

4.
A: Can she solve the problem?
B: _____, she _____ . It looks difficult.

*Bonjour! (프랑스어) 안녕하세요!

Unit 2 may

⭐ may는 허락의 의미를 나타내는 조동사로, '~해도 된다'라는 뜻이 있어요. 조동사 may는 혼자 쓰일 수 없고, 항상 동사원형과 함께 쓰여요.

주어 + may + 동사원형

You may play with your friends.   너는 친구들이랑 놀아도 돼.

He may leave early.   그는 일찍 떠나도 돼.

⭐ 조동사 may의 부정문은 may 뒤에 not을 붙이고, '~하면 안 된다'라는 뜻을 나타내요.

주어 + may not + 동사원형

You may not take pictures in this gallery.
당신은 이 전시장 안에서 사진을 찍을 수 없습니다.

The students may not use their cellphones in class.
학생들은 수업 시간에 그들의 휴대전화를 사용하면 안 된다.

⭐ 조동사 may의 의문문은 May로 문장을 시작하고, '~해도 될까요?'라는 뜻을 나타내요. 질문에 대한 대답은 <Yes, 주어 + may.>나 <No, 주어 + may not.>으로 써요.

May + 주어 + 동사원형 ~?

May I borrow this book?   ➡ Yes, you may. 그래, 그렇게 해. / No, you may not. 아니, 그럴 수 없어.
내가 이 책을 빌려도 될까?

Tip may는 '~일지도 모른다'라는 뜻으로 추측을 나타낼 때 사용되기도 해요.
It <u>may</u> rain soon. 아마 곧 비가 올 거야.   They <u>may</u> be late. 그들은 아마 늦을 거야.

차곡차곡 기초 다지기

조동사 may 뒤에 오는 알맞은 형태를 모두 찾아 동그라미 하세요.

	drank	listen	begin	opened
may +	sleeps	painted	cooked	come
	talks	sat	open	uses
	played	visit	asked	have

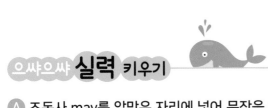

으쌰으쌰 실력 키우기

Ⓐ 조동사 may를 알맞은 자리에 넣어 문장을 다시 쓰세요.

1. The dog eats bones. ➔ _____

2. You play in the water. ➔ _____

3. Hanna goes to the concert. ➔ _____

4. Ron plays soccer. ➔ _____

5. They open the box. ➔ _____

6. He bakes cookies. ➔ _____

Ⓑ 다음 긍정문을 괄호 안의 형태에 맞게 바꿔 쓰세요.

1. I may sit here. ➔ _____ (의문문)

2. They may use this door. ➔ _____ (부정문)

3. I may help you. ➔ _____ (의문문)

4. Visitors may feed the animals. ➔ _____ (부정문)

Ⓒ 단어를 바르게 배열하여 문장을 완성하세요.

1. A: join / I / you / may   B: Yes, you may.
   ➔ _____

2. A: not / in the hallways / may / you / run   B: Sorry.
   ➔ _____

3. A: we / may / television / watch   B: Yes, you may.
   ➔ _____

4. A: wear / I / may / boots   B: No, you may not.
   ➔ _____

Unit 3 must, should

 must는 '~해야 한다'라는 뜻의 조동사예요. 규칙으로 정해진 사항이나 의무, 명령과 같이 강한 지시를 나타낼 때 사용해요.

긍정문	주어 + must + 동사원형 (반드시 ~해야 한다)	We must be quiet at the library. 우리는 도서관에서 반드시 조용히 해야 해. Joe must practice the piano. 조는 반드시 피아노 연습을 해야 해.
부정문	주어 + must not + 동사원형 (절대로 ~해서는 안 된다)	You must not throw trash on the ground. 당신은 길에 절대로 쓰레기를 버려서는 안 됩니다. You must not park here. 당신은 여기에 절대로 주차해선 안 됩니다.

Tip must와 같은 뜻의 표현으로 have to가 있어요. 긍정문에서는 must를 have to로 바꿔 쓸 수 있지만, 부정문에서는 '~할 필요가 없다'라는 다른 뜻이 된다는 것을 기억하세요.

You must(= have to) finish your homework. 너는 숙제를 끝내야 해.

부정문 You must not read this book. 너는 절대 이 책을 읽어서는 안 돼.
You don't have to read this book. 너는 이 책을 읽을 필요가 없어.

 should도 '~해야 한다'라는 뜻의 조동사이지만, must보다 강도가 약한 의무를 나타내며 조언이나 권유, 제안의 의미를 포함하고 있어요.

긍정문	주어 + should + 동사원형 (~해야 한다, ~하는 게 좋겠다)	I should study harder. 나는 더 열심히 공부해야 해. She should sleep now. 그녀는 지금 자야 해.
부정문	주어 + should not + 동사원형 (~해서는 안 된다, ~하지 않는 게 좋겠다)	You should not watch that TV show. 너는 저 TV 프로그램을 시청해서는 안 돼. You should not yell. 너는 소리지르면 안 돼.

차곡차곡 기초 다지기

다음 조동사 뒤에 올 수 있는 알맞은 형태에 동그라미 하세요.

1. must watches | watch   2. should take | took   3. must is | be

4. should sleeps | sleep   5. have to clean | cleans   6. should played | play

7. must say | says   8. should drank | drink   9. have to cook | cooks

A 빈칸에 알맞은 말을 골라 넣어 문장을 완성하세요.

should read   should talk   have to find   must not take   must be

1. We _____ quiet in the classroom.   우리는 교실 안에서 반드시 조용히 해야 해.

2. You _____ to your teacher.   너는 너희 선생님과 이야기를 해야 해.

3. I _____ my key.   나는 반드시 내 열쇠를 찾아야 해.

4. Sean _____ more books.   션은 더 많은 책을 읽어야 해.

5. Visitors _____ pictures.   방문자들은 절대로 사진을 찍으면 안 됩니다.

B 다음 긍정문을 부정문으로 바꿔 쓰세요.

1. I should finish my homework.   ➡ _____

2. They must drink milk.   ➡ _____

3. She should stay home today.   ➡ _____

4. I have to sleep on the sofa.   ➡ _____

C 단어를 바르게 배열하여 문장을 완성하세요.

1. try / they / bibimbap / should   그들은 비빔밥을 먹어봐야 해.
   ➡ _____

2. not / must / you / tell a lie   너는 절대 거짓말을 해서는 안 돼.
   ➡ _____

3. school uniforms / must / all students / wear   모든 학생들은 교복을 입어야 해.
   ➡ _____

4. not / should / we / drive / fast   우리는 운전을 빨리 해서는 안 돼.
   ➡ _____

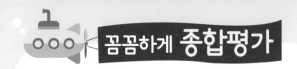

1. 다음 중 조동사에 대한 설명으로 <u>틀린</u> 것을 고르세요.

① 조동사는 동사를 도와주는 동사이다.
② can, may, must, should는 조동사이다.
③ 조동사는 혼자 쓸 수 있다.
④ 조동사 뒤에는 동사원형이 온다.
⑤ 조동사는 긍정문, 부정문, 의문문에서 쓸 수 있다.

2. 다음 중 can의 쓰임이 바르지 <u>않은</u> 문장을 고르세요.

① I can make spaghetti.
② You can't walk to the city hall.
③ Can you play basketball?
④ Mary can writes Korean.
⑤ The dog can jump high.

3. 다음 중 may의 쓰임이 바른 문장을 고르세요.

① May I talk to Soojung?
② They may came to the party.
③ He may goes outside.
④ You go may home.
⑤ You may standing up.

4. 다음 중 must의 쓰임이 바르지 <u>않은</u> 문장을 고르세요.

① You must finish your work.
② Harold must eat more vegetables.
③ You must stop at the red light.
④ Sandy must meets her friends.
⑤ People must sleep at night.

5. 다음 중 should의 쓰임이 바른 문장을 고르세요.

① John should visits his grandparents.
② You should return not the book.
③ Chloe should wash her hands.
④ We not should forget our history.
⑤ Should I saved water?

[6~9] 빈칸에 알맞은 말을 고르세요.

6. We _____ be honest.
우리는 반드시 정직해야 해.
① can   ② may   ③ must
④ have   ⑤ are

7. _____ I ask a question?
제가 질문을 해도 될까요?
① May   ② Must   ③ Should
④ Will   ⑤ Do

8. You _____ brush your teeth.
너는 이를 닦아야 해.
① can   ② should   ③ may
④ have   ⑤ are

9. Randy _____ speak two languages.
랜디는 두 가지 언어를 말할 수 있다.
① must   ② should   ③ can
④ have to   ⑤ is

[10~15] 단어를 바르게 배열하여 문장을 완성하세요.

10. exercise   regularly   should   You

➡ _____

11. ride   Andy   a bicycle   may

➡ _____

12. can't | a computer | He | use

➡ _____

13. must | seat belts | Children | wear

➡ _____

14. I | come in | May

➡ _____

15. junk food | eat | shouldn't | You

➡ _____

[16~17] 다음 질문에 알맞은 대답을 고르세요.

16. Can he drive a bus?
① Yes, he should.
② Yes, you may.
③ No, he can't.
④ No, he may not.
⑤ Yes, he does.

17. May I drink some milk?
① Yes, you must.
② No, you aren't.
③ Yes, I can.
④ No, you shouldn't.
⑤ Yes, you may.

[18~21] 다음 문장에서 틀린 부분을 찾아 바르게 고쳐 쓰세요.

18. Larry can understands me.

➡ _____

19. You should more water drink.

➡ _____

20. They come may to the party.

➡ _____

21. She must practices hard.

➡ _____

[22~25] 빈칸에 알맞은 말을 골라 넣어 글을 완성하세요.

| must follow | may not |
| should wear | can dance |

Jenny ²² _____ ballet. She has a ballet class on Friday. She ²³ _____ toe shoes. She ²⁴ _____ talk in class. She ²⁵ _____ her teacher's directions well.

*toe shoes 토 슈즈(발레 슈즈)
*direction 지시, 지휘

Chapter 10
동명사와 to부정사

Joy 쌤

Hey, Minho. 너는 뭘 하는 걸 좋아해?

Minho

전 노래하는 걸 좋아해요. I like sing.

Joy 쌤

like도 동사, sing도 동사라서 I like sing.이라는 말은
잘못된 문장이야. 대신 동사 sing 뒤에 -ing를 붙여서
명사 역할을 하게 만들 수 있어.
I like singing. 나는 노래하는 것을 좋아해.

Minho

아하! 동사 뒤에 -ing를 붙이면
동사를 명사처럼 쓸 수 있군요.

Joy 쌤

맞아. 또 다른 방법도 알려줄까?
동사 앞에 to라는 단어를 붙여도 동사가 명사처럼 바뀌어.
I like to sing. 나는 노래하는 것을 좋아해.

Minho

동사 앞에 to를 붙이기만 하면 되네요!
와, 신기해요.

Joy 쌤

생각보다 쉽지? It is easy.

Unit 1 동명사

⭐ 동명사는 동사를 명사로 바꾼 것을 말해요. 동사원형에 -ing를 붙이면 '~하는 것', '~하기'라는 뜻의 동명사로 변신해요. 동명사는 문장에서 주어나 목적어, 보어*로 사용할 수 있어요.

주어	Baking is my hobby. 베이킹은 내 취미야. Playing soccer is exciting. 축구 경기를 하는 것은 신나. Telling a lie is bad. 거짓말하는 것은 나빠.
목적어	I enjoy swimming. 나는 수영하는 것을 즐겨. They like eating ice cream. 그들은 아이스크림 먹는 것을 좋아해. Megan practices speaking Korean. 메간은 한국어 말하는 것을 연습해.
보어	My dream is making music. 내 꿈은 음악을 만드는 거야. Today's plan is visiting Harvard University. 오늘의 계획은 하버드 대학에 방문하는 거야. Alan's job is teaching young children. 앨런의 직업은 아이들을 가르치는 거야.

*보어는 주어나 목적어를 보충하여 설명하는 단어예요.

Tip 문장에 -ing가 있다고 해서 모두 동명사는 아니에요. 현재진행형도 동명사와 마찬가지로 -ing를 붙여서 만든 것 기억하나요? 현재진행형은 〈be동사 + 동사원형-ing〉 형태예요.

I am playing with my friends. 나는 내 친구들과 놀고 있어.

▶ 동사원형에 -ing를 붙이는 법은 p.70을 참고하세요.

 치곡치곡 **기초** 다지기

다음 동사원형을 동명사로 바꿔 쓰세요.

1. kick ➡ _____   2. run ➡ _____   3. go ➡ _____

4. ride ➡ _____   5. meet ➡ _____   6. win ➡ _____

7. tell ➡ _____   8. draw ➡ _____   9. save ➡ _____

 **실력** 키우기

Ⓐ 다음 문장에서 동명사를 찾아 동그라미 한 후, 우리말 뜻을 쓰세요.

1. I love traveling by train. → _____

2. Eating breakfast is important. → _____

3. My hobby is listening to music. → _____

4. Studying science is difficult. → _____

Ⓑ 동명사가 주어, 목적어, 보어 중 어떤 역할로 쓰였는지 구분하세요.

1. My uncle goes fishing on Saturdays. → _____

2. Shane's job is delivering pizza. → _____

3. Hiking is good for your health. → _____

4. I like cleaning cars. → _____

5. Playing the guitar is so fun. → _____

6. Our goal is winning the game. → _____

Ⓒ 빈칸에 알맞은 동사를 골라 동명사 형태로 바꿔 쓰세요.

1. I enjoy _____ history books.
   나는 역사책 읽는 것을 즐긴다.

2. Shakespeare finished _____ some new poems.
   셰익스피어는 새로운 시 몇 작품을 쓰는 것을 마쳤다.

3. Her hobby is _____ postage stamps.
   그녀의 취미는 우표들을 모으는 것이다.

4. _____ good friends is very important.
   좋은 친구들을 만드는 것은 아주 중요하다.

collect
make
read
write

Unit 2 to부정사

⭐ 동사 앞에 to를 붙인 것을 to부정사라고 하는데, 여러 가지 품사로 변신할 수 있어요. <to + 동사원형> 형태로 명사, 형용사, 부사로 사용할 수 있어요.

명사 (~하는 것)	To learn English is helpful. 영어를 배우는 것은 유익해. 　　주어 I like to swim. 나는 수영하는 것을 좋아해. 　　목적어 My dream is to travel the world. 내 꿈은 세계를 여행하는 거야. 　　보어
형용사 (~하는, ~할)	I have a book to read. 나는 읽으려는 책이 있어. 　　명사 수식 Maya brought some water to drink. 마야는 마실 물을 가지고 왔어. 　　명사 수식
부사 (목적: ~하기 위해 원인: ~해서 조건: ~하기에)	My friend came to see me. 내 친구가 나를 보기 위해 왔어. 　　동사 수식 I am happy to meet you. 너를 만나서 기뻐. 　　형용사 수식 The park is good to walk. 그 공원은 걷기에 좋아. 　　형용사 수식

Tip 문장에 to가 있다고 해서 모두 to부정사인 것은 아니니 주의해야 해요. 바로 '~에'라는 뜻이 있는 전치사 to인 경우도 있어요. 전치사 to 뒤에는 장소를 나타내는 명사가 와요.

Jeff and I went to the library yesterday. 제프와 나는 어제 도서관에 갔어.
I go to school in the morning. 나는 아침에 학교에 가.

 차곡차곡 **기초** 다지기

다음 중 to부정사의 to 뒤에 오는 것에 동그라미 하세요.

1. to　friend | run | me

2. to　I | question | ask

3. to　exam | take | so

4. to　school | he | go

5. to　see | you | happy

6. to　swim | good | lake

A 밑줄 친 to부정사가 꾸미는 말을 찾아 화살표로 연결하세요.

1. I studied hard <u>to pass</u> the exam.
2. Sally has snacks <u>to eat</u>.
3. We are glad <u>to see</u> you.
4. I need crayons <u>to draw</u>.
5. This book is fun <u>to read</u>.
6. He came <u>to see</u> us.

B to부정사가 명사, 형용사, 부사 중 어떤 품사로 쓰였는지 구분하세요.

1. I have time to talk. ➔ _____
2. This museum is great to visit. ➔ _____
3. My father's dream was to be a soccer player. ➔ _____
4. I am excited to win the game. ➔ _____
5. We have homework to finish. ➔ _____
6. To learn to swim is necessary. ➔ _____

C 빈칸에 알맞은 동사를 골라 to부정사 형태로 바꿔 쓰세요.

meet   eat   write   run   ride   say

1. My dog likes _____. 내 개는 달리는 것을 좋아한다.
2. Dinner is ready _____. 저녁 식사가 먹을 수 있도록 준비되었다.
3. It is the new bike _____. 그것은 탈 새 자전거이다.
4. _____ sorry is important. 미안하다고 말하는 것은 중요하다.
5. We are happy _____ you. 우리는 너를 만나서 기뻐.
6. The teacher needed a pen _____. 그 선생님은 쓸 펜이 필요했다.

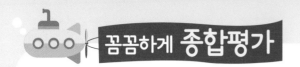

1. 다음 중 동명사에 대한 설명으로 <u>틀린</u> 것을 고르세요.

① 동명사는 명사를 동사로 바꾼 것이다.
② 동명사는 〈동사원형 + -ing〉로 만든다.
③ 동명사는 동사를 명사로 바꾼 것이다.
④ 동명사는 문장에서 주어, 목적어, 보어 역할을 한다.
⑤ 현재진행형의 -ing와 동명사의 -ing는 역할이 다르다.

2. 다음 중 to부정사에 대한 설명으로 <u>틀린</u> 것을 고르세요.

① to부정사는 정해진 품사가 없다.
② to부정사는 〈to + 동사원형〉으로 만든다.
③ to부정사는 to를 부정하는 역할을 한다.
④ to부정사는 명사, 형용사, 부사로 쓰일 수 있다.
⑤ to부정사의 to는 전치사 to와 역할이 다르다.

3. 다음 중 동명사가 쓰인 문장을 고르세요.

① They are drawing in art class.
② Susie is doing her homework.
③ He is drinking water.
④ Andrew started studying last night.
⑤ I am reading the book.

4. 다음 중 to부정사가 쓰인 문장을 고르세요.

① I went to the library yesterday.
② The cat ran to the door.
③ Mia is happy to see you.
④ They flew to France.
⑤ We drove to the school.

5. 다음 중 동명사의 쓰임이 바르지 <u>않은</u> 문장을 고르세요.

① Cleaning your room is very important.
② We stopped talking.
③ My father making dinner loves.
④ I like drinking iced water.
⑤ Jiwon finished solving the problem.

6. 다음 중 to부정사의 쓰임이 <u>다른</u> 문장을 고르세요.

① Edison liked to work.
② I am glad to hear the news.
③ I came to see you.
④ This place is good to take pictures.
⑤ Victor practices hard to win the race.

[7~11] 빈칸에 알맞은 말을 고르세요.

7. He ran _____ the bus.
그는 그 버스를 타기 위해 달렸다.
① to wait   ② to take   ③ to drive
④ to walk   ⑤ to see

8. The birds like _____ high.
그 새들은 높이 나는 것을 좋아한다.
① singing   ② playing   ③ working
④ flying   ⑤ eating

9. Her hobby is _____ a horse.
그녀의 취미는 말을 타는 것이다.
① climbing   ② speaking   ③ riding
④ running   ⑤ making

10. Bridges are built _____ rivers.
다리는 강을 건너기 위해 지어졌다.
① to cross   ② to give   ③ to build
④ to watch   ⑤ to pull

11. I don't like _____ at a gym.
나는 헬스장에서 운동하는 것을 좋아하지 않는다.
① sleeping   ② making   ③ going
④ exercising   ⑤ swimming

[12~13] 우리말과 같은 뜻의 문장을 고르세요.

12. 방문할 좋은 장소들이 많이 있다.

① There are to many places visit.
② There are many places visit to.
③ There are many places visit.
④ There are many places to visit.
⑤ There are to visit many places.

13. 그릇을 닦는 것은 내 일이다.

① Wash dishes is my job.
② Washing dishes is my job.
③ To washing dishes is my job.
④ Washes dishes is my job.
⑤ Dishes washing is my job.

[14~17] 다음 문장에서 **틀린** 부분을 찾아 바르게 고쳐 쓰세요.

14. The children started to played baseball.
그 아이들은 야구 경기하는 것을 시작했다.

➡ _____

15. Read English newspaper is interesting.
영어 신문을 읽는 것은 흥미롭다.

➡ _____

16. She likes to plays the guitar.
그녀는 기타 연주하는 것을 좋아한다.

➡ _____

17. The famer has many apples sells to.
그 농부는 판매할 사과를 많이 갖고 있다.

➡ _____

[18~21] 단어를 바르게 배열하여 문장을 완성하세요.

18. | fun | is | Playing | chess |

➡ _____

19. | swimming | enjoy | We | in summer |

➡ _____

20. | to read | have | a book | I |

➡ _____

21. | coins | The boy | to collect | likes |

➡ _____

[22~25] 빈칸에 알맞은 말을 골라 넣어 글을 완성하세요.

| to use | working | to draw | enjoys |

Jenny likes art class. She likes ²² _____ flowers. She ²³ _____ painting pictures. She has new watercolors ²⁴ _____ . She loves ²⁵ _____ on her art.

Chapter 11

접속사와 명령문

꼼꼼하게 종합평가

Minho

Ms. Joy, are you there? I have a question.

Joy 쌤

Good morning, Minho. What's your question?

Minho

'나는 축구를 해서 피곤했어.' 이걸 영어로 어떻게 말해요?
I played soccer tired.
제가 생각해도 이건 아닌 것 같아요.

Joy 쌤

'나는 축구를 했어. [그래서] 나는 피곤했어.'
이렇게 두 문장을 접속사로 연결해야 해.
I played soccer, so I was tired.라고 하면 돼.

Minho

아, 여기서 so가 바로 접속사군요!

Joy 쌤

맞아. 이 외에도 and(그리고), but(그러나), or(또는),
because(왜냐하면)와 같은 접속사가 있는데 알려줄게.
그리고 앞에서 배운 명령문에 대해서도 자세히 공부해보자!

Unit 1 접속사

⭐ 접속사는 같은 품사의 단어들이나 구, 문장들을 서로 연결하는 역할을 해요.

and	그리고, ~와	These are grapes and peaches. 이것들은 포도와 복숭아야. She is a teacher, and he is a scientist. 그녀는 선생님이고 그는 과학자야.
but	그러나, 하지만	He is tired but happy. 그는 피곤하지만 행복해. Kayla likes math, but Andrew doesn't like it. 카일라는 수학을 좋아하지만 앤드류는 수학을 좋아하지 않아.
or	아니면, 또는	Do you like this or that? 너는 이것이 좋아, 아니면 저것이 좋아? Are we going to the beach or to the park? 우리는 해변에 가는 거야, 아니면 공원에 가는 거야?
so	그래서	It is rainy, so we will stay at home. 비가 와서 우리는 집에 머물 거야. He found the lost coin, so he was very happy. 그는 잃어버린 동전을 찾아서 무척 기뻤어.
because	왜냐하면, ~ 때문에	I drank water because I was thirsty. 나는 목이 말라서 물을 마셨어. Sangho didn't go to school because he was sick. 상호는 아파서 학교에 가지 않았어.

Tip
• and는 서로 비슷한 내용을 연결할 때, but은 서로 반대되는 내용을 연결할 때, or는 둘 중 선택할 때 써요.

• so는 결과, because는 원인이나 이유를 나타내요.

He was sleepy, so he went to bed. 그는 졸렸어. 그래서 그는 자러 갔어.
　　원인·이유　　　　결과

He went to bed because he was sleepy. 그는 자러 갔어. 왜냐하면 그는 졸렸기 때문이야.
　결과　　　　　　원인·이유

차곡차곡 기초 다지기

알맞은 단어를 써서 퍼즐을 완성하세요.

1. 왜냐하면
2. 아니면

3. 그러나
4. 그리고
5. 그래서

1 3			4		
				5	
				2	

A 다음 중 알맞은 접속사에 동그라미 하세요.

1. Do you want to drink lemonade   or   so   iced water?

2. Sofia enjoys swimming   but   and   hiking.

3. Jay played hard,   so   because   he was tired.

4. My mom likes dogs,   but   and   she doesn't like cats.

5. I washed my hands   or   because   they weren't clean.

B 빈칸에 알맞은 접속사를 써서 문장을 완성하세요.

1. It was raining, _____ I didn't have an umbrella.   비가 왔지만 나는 우산이 없었다.

2. Joanne was late _____ she missed the bus.   조앤은 버스를 놓쳤기 때문에 늦었다.

3. It was very hot, _____ I had some ice cream.   너무 더워서 나는 아이스크림을 먹었다.

4. Is this mine _____ yours?   이거 내 거야, 아니면 네 거야?

5. This puppy feels soft _____ warm.   이 강아지는 부드럽고 따뜻한 느낌이다.

C 밑줄 친 접속사를 바르게 고쳐 문장을 다시 쓰세요.

1. I want a burger <u>but</u> French fries.   저는 햄버거와 감자튀김을 원해요.

   → _____

2. It Is cold, <u>because</u> I will wear a warm coat.   날씨가 추워서 나는 따뜻한 코트를 입을 것이다.

   → _____

3. Do you go to school by bus <u>so</u> on foot?   너는 학교에 버스를 타고 가니, 아니면 걸어가니?

   → _____

4. Jin passed the test <u>and</u> she studied hard.   진은 열심히 공부했기 때문에 시험에 합격했다.

   → _____

Unit 2 일반동사 명령문

⭐ 명령문은 상대방에게 '~해라/하지 마라'라고 명령하거나 요청하는 문장을 말해요. 일반동사 명령문은 동사로 문장을 시작하는데, 이때 동사는 반드시 동사원형을 써야 해요.

1. 긍정 명령문은 '~해라'라는 뜻으로, 동사원형으로 문장을 시작해요.

> **Close** the door. 문을 닫아라.
>
> **Open** your book. 책을 펴라.

 문장의 맨 앞이나 맨 뒤에 please를 붙이면 정중하게 요청하는 표현이 돼요. please를 문장 맨 뒤에 쓸 때는 쉼표(,)를 붙여요.

> **Please** sit down. 앉으세요.   Come here, **please**. 이쪽으로 오세요.

2. 부정 명령문은 '~하지 마라'라는 뜻으로, Do not으로 문장을 시작해요. Do not은 Don't로 줄여서 흔히 사용해요.

> **Do not** eat too much. 너무 많이 먹지 마.
>
> **Don't** cross at a red light. 빨간 불에 건너지 말아라.
>
> **Don't** feed the animals in the zoo. 동물원 안에 있는 동물들에게 먹이를 주지 마세요.

 명령문은 명령이나 요청을 하는 반면, Let's는 권유의 의미가 있어요. Let us의 줄임말인 Let's는 '우리가 ~하자'라는 뜻이고, Let's not은 '우리가 ~하지 말자'라는 뜻이에요. Let's나 Let's not 뒤에는 동사원형이 와요.

> Let's <u>sing</u> the song. 우리 그 노래를 부르자.
>   동사원형
>
> Let's not <u>worry</u> too much. 우리 너무 걱정하지 말자.
>   동사원형

차곡차곡 **기초** 다지기

다음 중 일반동사 명령문을 모두 찾아 V표 하세요.

I will see you later.	☐	Don't talk too fast.	☐
Good night.	☐	Go to bed.	☐
Do not take pictures in the museum.	☐	I don't like homework.	☐
We will have a test tomorrow.	☐	Wash your hands.	☐
Close the window, please.	☐	Is it your dog?	☐

으쌰으쌰 **실력** 키우기

Ⓐ 빈칸에 알맞은 단어를 골라 넣어 문장을 완성하세요.

call   wash   cry   come   look

1. Do not _____. 울지 마.

2. _____ at the sky. 하늘을 봐.

3. Please _____ early. 일찍 와주세요.

4. _____ me later. 나에게 이따 전화해.

5. _____ the dishes, please. 설거지를 해주세요.

Ⓑ 밑줄 친 부분을 바르게 고쳐 명령문으로 다시 쓰세요.

1. <u>Listening</u> to me.   ➡ _____

2. <u>Haved</u> a seat, please.   ➡ _____

3. <u>Do use not</u> plastic bags.   ➡ _____

4. <u>Brushes</u> your teeth.   ➡ _____

5. <u>Don't not</u> forget your homework.   ➡ _____

Ⓒ 그림을 보고 해당하는 명령문을 골라 번호를 쓰세요.

1.    2.

_____   _____

3.    4.

① Clean your room.
② Do not talk too loud.
③ Don't run on the wet floor.
④ Open the door.

_____   _____

Unit 3 be동사 명령문

⭐ be동사 명령문은 be동사와 형용사를 이용해 명령하거나 요청하는 문장이에요.

1. 긍정 명령문은 '~해'라는 뜻의 명령문으로 〈Be + 형용사〉 형태로 써요. 일반동사와 마찬가지로 be동사의 원형인 Be로 문장을 시작해요. 문장의 맨 앞이나 맨 뒤에 please를 붙이면 정중하게 요청하는 표현이 돼요.

Be careful. 조심해.

Be happy. 행복해라.

Be nice to your friends. 너의 친구들에게 친절히 대해라.

Please be quiet. 조용히 해 주세요.

2. 부정 명령문은 '~하지 마'라는 뜻의 명령문이에요. 일반동사 명령문과 마찬가지로 Don't로 문장을 시작하고 뒤에는 동사원형인 be를 써요.

Don't be lazy. 게으르게 굴지 마.

Don't be sad. 슬퍼하지 마.

Don't be late. 늦지 마.

Don't be afraid. 두려워하지 마.

Tip 접속사 and와 or가 명령문과 함께 쓰이면 어떤 뜻이 되는지 알아두세요.

Exercise every day, <u>and</u> you will be healthy. (and 그러면: **명령을 따를 경우**)
매일 운동해라, 그러면 너는 건강해질 거야.

Be careful, <u>or</u> you will be hurt.   (or 그렇지 않으면: **명령을 안 따를 경우**)
조심해라, 그렇지 않으면 너는 다칠 거야.

차곡차곡 **기초** 다지기

다음 중 be동사 명령문을 모두 찾아 V표 하세요.

Be kind.	☐	We will be home soon.	☐
What are you doing?	☐	Don't be scared.	☐
They are good friends.	☐	She will be a scientist.	☐
Be quiet, please.	☐	Please don't be angry.	☐
She is selfish.	☐	Be honest.	☐

으쌰으쌰 실력 키우기

A 우리말 뜻을 읽고 알맞은 말을 연결해 명령문을 완성하세요.

1. 친근하게 대해라.	→ Be •	• ready.
2. 긴장하지 마.	→ Don't be •	• silly.
3. 부끄러워하지 마.	→ Don't be •	• nervous.
4. 예의바르게 해라.	→ Please be •	• friendly.
5. 바보 같이 굴지 마.	→ Don't be •	• shy.
6. 준비해라.	→ Be •	• polite.

B 단어를 바르게 배열하여 문장을 완성하세요.

1. patient, / please / be → _____

   인내심을 가지세요.

2. be / upset / don't → _____

   화내지 마.

3. careful / be → _____

   조심해.

4. don't / rude / be → _____

   무례하게 굴지 마.

5. to / people / be / kind → _____

   사람들에게 친절히 대해라.

C 그림을 보고 해당하는 명령문을 골라 번호를 쓰세요.

1.

2.

_____   _____

3.

4.

_____   _____

① Don't be sick.
② Be brave.
③ Don't be late.
④ Be happy.

1. 다음 중 접속사에 대한 설명으로 <u>틀린</u> 것을 고르세요.
   ① 접속사는 단어와 단어를 연결하는 역할을 한다.
   ② and, but, or, so, because는 접속사이다.
   ③ or는 '아니면'이라는 뜻이다.
   ④ and는 '그리고', but은 '그러나'라는 뜻이다.
   ⑤ 문장과 문장은 접속사로 연결할 수 없다.

2. 다음 중 명령문에 대한 설명으로 <u>틀린</u> 것을 고르세요.
   ① 명령문은 요청을 할 때 쓸 수 있다.
   ② 명령문은 지시를 할 때 쓸 수 있다.
   ③ 명령문은 주어로 문장을 시작한다.
   ④ 명령문은 동사원형으로 문장을 시작한다.
   ⑤ 명령문에 please를 붙이면 공손한 표현이 된다.

3. 다음 중 접속사가 쓰이지 <u>않은</u> 문장을 고르세요.
   ① Do you want apple or banana?
   ② This is a letter to send to John.
   ③ Tom cried because he was sick.
   ④ They liked the table but didn't buy it.
   ⑤ I was tired, so I took a nap.

4. 다음 중 명령문을 고르세요.
   ① The children rode on a train.
   ② They will see me.
   ③ What a nice day!
   ④ Don't be afraid.
   ⑤ Are they at the zoo?

[5~8] 빈칸에 알맞은 접속사를 고르세요.

5. Jade was happy _____ it was her birthday yesterday.
   어제는 제이드의 생일이었기 때문에 그녀는 행복했다.
   ① and   ② but
   ③ or   ④ so
   ⑤ because

6. Silvia is a good swimmer, _____ she doesn't swim often.
   실비아는 수영을 잘하지만 자주 하지는 않는다.
   ① and   ② but
   ③ or   ④ so
   ⑤ because

7. I may stop by tomorrow _____ phone you. 내가 내일까지 들르거나 전화할게.
   ① and   ② but
   ③ or   ④ so
   ⑤ because

8. I play the piano, _____ my brother plays the guitar.
   나는 피아노를 치고 우리 형은 기타를 친다.
   ① and   ② but
   ③ or   ④ so
   ⑤ because

[9~10] 우리말과 같은 뜻의 문장을 고르세요.

9. 그것에 손대지 마.
   ① To not touch it.
   ② Be not touch it.
   ③ Touch not it.
   ④ Do not touch it.
   ⑤ Does not touch it.

10. 강해져라.
    ① So strong.
    ② Be strong.
    ③ Do strong.
    ④ Be not strong.
    ⑤ Strong.

[11~15] 다음 문장에서 틀린 부분을 찾아 바르게 고쳐 쓰세요.

11. We finished dinner so ate ice cream.
우리는 저녁을 먹고 아이스크림을 먹었다.

→ _____

12. Don't be worry. 걱정하지 마.

→ _____

13. Be your best. 최선을 다해라.

→ _____

14. Is it a tiger and a lion?
그것은 호랑이니, 아니면 사자니?

→ _____

15. Do honest to yourself. 너 자신에게 정직해라.

→ _____

[16~18] 괄호 안의 접속사를 넣어 두 문장을 연결하여 쓰세요.

16. I was cold.
I wore a jacket. (so)

→ _____

17. I like my dog.
It's lovely. (because)

→ _____

18. They are my neighbors.
I don't know them well. (but)

→ _____

[19~21] 단어를 바르게 배열하여 문장을 완성하세요.

19. carefully Listen please

→ _____

20. rude be Don't

→ _____

21. me Don't forget

→ _____

[22~25] 빈칸에 알맞은 단어를 골라 넣어 글을 완성하세요.

| put   turn   wait   and |

Jenny baked a pizza yesterday. It was easy
22 _____ fun This is the recipe, 23
on the oven. 24 _____ the pizza in the oven.
25 _____ for 15 minutes. Jenny shared the
pizza with her brother.

*recipe 조리법

Chapter 12

의문사

꼼꼼하게 종합평가

Joy 쌤

Minho, what is your hobby?
When is your birthday?
Where do you live?
How tall are you?
Why do you learn English?
Who is your teacher?

Minho

Wow! 😮 선생님, 질문을 왜 이렇게 많이 하세요?

Joy 쌤

이번 챕터에서는 육하원칙을 이용해서 이렇게
다양한 질문을 만드는 방법을 알려줄게.

who(누가), when(언제), where(어디서), what(무엇을), how(어떻게),
why(왜)를 의문사라고 하는데, 다양한 의문문을 만드는 데 쓰여.

또, which와 whose라는 의문사도 알려줄게.
알아두면 유용한 의문사들이야.

Minho

육하원칙을 이용한 질문 만들기, 어서 알려주세요!

Joy 쌤

마지막 챕터도 열심히 해보자! 모르는 거 있으면 언제든 물어봐,
알겠지? 😊 자, 그럼 시작해볼까?

Unit 1 what, which

⭐ 의문사는 '누가', '언제', '어디서', '무엇을', '어떻게', '왜' 하고 궁금한 것을 물어볼 때 사용해요.

Who is he? 그는 누구니?   What is this? 이것은 무엇이니?

⭐ '무엇'에 대해 물어볼 때는 의문사 what, 정해진 범위에서 '어떤 것'에 대해 물어볼 때는 의문사 which를 사용해 질문해요. 의문사는 문장의 맨 앞에 오고, 의문사가 있는 의문문에 대한 대답은 yes나 no로 하지 않아요.

> **What/Which + be동사 + 주어 ~?**

A: What is your name? 네 이름은 뭐니?   B: My name is Jiho. 내 이름은 지호야.

A: Which is your bicycle?   B: The blue bicycle is mine.
어떤 게 너의 자전거야?   파란 자전거가 내 거야.

> **What/Which + do + 주어 + 동사원형 ~?**

A: What do you want to eat?   B: I want to eat a hamburger.
너는 무엇을 먹고 싶니?   난 햄버거를 먹고 싶어.

A: Which do you like better, this or that?   B: I like this.
너는 어떤 것이 더 좋니, 이것 아니면 저것?   나는 이게 더 좋아.

⭐ 어떤 대상을 더 구체적으로 묻는 경우 what이나 which 뒤에 명사를 넣어요.

A: What time is it? 몇 시야?   B: It is 2:05. 2시 5분이야.

A: What color do you like? 너는 무슨 색깔을 좋아하니?   B: I like navy. 나는 남색을 좋아해.

A: Which flower is this, a rose or a daisy?   B: This is a rose.
이것은 어떤 꽃이야, 장미야 아니면 데이지야?   이것은 장미야.

 차곡차곡 **기초** 다지기

우리말 뜻을 읽고 알맞은 의문사에 동그라미 하세요.

1. 무슨 요일이니?   What | Which day is it?

2. 너는 닭고기와 생선 중 어떤 음식을 좋아하니? What | Which food do you like, chicken or fish?

3. 네가 제일 좋아하는 계절은 무엇이니?   What | Which is your favorite season?

4. 지구와 태양 중 어떤 게 더 클까?   What | Which is bigger, the earth or the sun?

으쌰으쌰 **실력** 키우기

Ⓐ 빈칸에 what과 which 중 알맞은 것을 쓰세요.

1. _____ animal is that?

2. _____ do you like better, this or that?

3. _____ fruit do you like, mangos or peaches?

4. _____ size are these shoes?

Ⓑ 그림을 보고 빈칸에 알맞은 단어를 골라 넣어 문장을 완성하세요.

1.  What _____ is it?

2.  Which _____ is hers?

3.  What _____ is it?

4.  Which _____ do you like better, soccer or basketball?

time
backpack
sport
color

Ⓒ 다음 질문에 알맞은 대답을 연결하세요.

1. What are you doing?　　　　　•　　　• A chair is heavier.

2. Which hat is yours?　　　　　•　　　• I like this book.

3. Which book do you like, this or that? •　　• The red hat is mine.

4. What is your hobby?　　　　　•　　　• Today is Thursday.

5. What day is it today?　　　　•　　　• I'm doing my homework.

6. Which is heavier, a chair or a pen? •　　• My hobby is riding a bicycle.

Unit 2 who, whose

★ 어떤 사람이 누구인지 물어볼 때는 의문사 who를 써요.

Who + be동사 + 주어 ~?

A: Who is she? 그녀는 누구니?

B: She is my mom. 그녀는 나의 엄마야.

A: Who is reading a book?
누가 책을 읽고 있니?

B: Jane is reading a book.
제인이 책을 읽고 있어.

A: Who was at the playground?
놀이터에 누가 있었니?

B: Tom was at the playground.
톰이 놀이터에 있었어.

Who + do + 주어 + 동사원형 ~?

A: Who do you like?
너는 누구를 좋아하니?

B: I like my English teacher.
나는 영어 선생님을 좋아해.

A: Who do you know in this movie?
너는 이 영화에서 누구를 아니?

B: I know the main actor.
나는 주연 배우를 알아.

 어떤 사물이 누구의 것인지 물어볼 때는 whose를 쓰는데, whose 뒤에는 명사가 와요.

Whose + 명사 + be동사 + 주어 ~?

A: Whose book is this? 이것은 누구의 책이니?

B: It is John's. 그것은 존의 것이야.

A: Whose dolls are these?
이것들은 누구의 인형들이니?

B: These are Minhee's.
이것들은 민희의 것이야.

A: Whose birthday is it today?
오늘은 누구의 생일이니?

B: It is Julia's birthday.
줄리아의 생일이야.

차곡차곡 기초 다지기

의문사 who, whose가 바르게 쓰인 의문문을 모두 찾아 V표 하세요.

Who party is it? ☐

Who shoes are these? ☐

Who is he? ☐

Whose umbrella is this? ☐

Who watch is that? ☐

Who is your friend? ☐

Whose do you like? ☐

Whose pen is on the table? ☐

으쌰으쌰 **실력** 키우기

A 빈칸에 who와 whose 중 알맞은 것을 쓰세요.

1. _____ house is this?

2. _____ birthday is it today?

3. _____ is making dinner?

4. _____ is the man at the office?

B 단어를 바르게 배열하여 문장을 완성하세요.

1. Janet / who / is   →   _____
   누가 자넷이니?

2. are / whose / they / parents   →   _____
   그들은 누구의 부모님이니?

3. they / are / who   →   _____
   그들은 누구니?

4. is / who / taking / pictures   →   _____
   누가 사진을 찍고 있니?

5. those / crayons / whose / are   →   _____
   저것들은 누구의 크레용이니?

6. car / it / is / whose   →   _____
   그것은 누구의 자동차니?

C 다음 질문에 알맞은 대답을 연결하세요.

1. Whose brother is he?   •   • Jay is late.

2. Who is playing the guitar?   •   • Philip is at the office.

3. Who is late?   •   • He is my brother.

4. Whose notebook is this?   •   • Amy is playing the guitar.

5. Whose idea is it?   •   • It's her idea.

6. Who is at the office?   •   • It is Michelle's.

Unit 3 when, where

⭐ 어떤 일이 언제 일어나는지 시간을 물어볼 때는 '언제'라는 뜻의 의문사 when을 사용해요.

> When + be동사 + 주어 ~?

A: When is your birthday? 네 생일은 언제니? B: My birthday is May 14th. 내 생일은 5월 14일이야.

> When + do + 주어 + 동사원형 ~?

A: When do you exercise?
너는 언제 운동을 하니?

B: I exercise in the morning.
나는 아침에 운동해.

> When + 조동사 + 주어 + 동사원형 ~?

A: When can we meet?
우리가 언제 만날 수 있을까?

B: We can meet on Friday.
우리는 금요일에 만날 수 있어.

⭐ 사람이나 사물이 어디에 있는지 장소를 물어볼 때는 '어디(에)'라는 뜻의 의문사 where를 사용해요.

> Where + be동사 + 주어 ~?

A: Where are you? 너 어디에 있니? B: I'm at the library. 나는 도서관에 있어.

> Where + do + 주어 + 동사원형 ~?

A: Where do you live? 너 어디 사니? B: I live in Washington D.C. 나는 워싱턴 DC에 살아.

> Where + 조동사 + 주어 + 동사원형 ~?

A: Where will you go this weekend?
너는 이번 주말에 어디에 갈 거니?

B: I will go to the zoo this weekend.
나는 이번 주말에 동물원에 갈 거야.

차곡차곡 기초 다지기

의문사 when, where가 바르게 쓰인 의문문을 모두 찾아 V표 하세요.

When does the movie start? ☐   Where is lunchtime? ☐

Where is your birthday? ☐   Where is Mom? ☐

When is the playground? ☐   When is the bank? ☐

When is the vacation? ☐   Where is your school? ☐

으쌰으쌰 **실력** 키우기

A 빈칸에 when과 where 중 알맞은 것을 쓰세요.

1. _____ is your dad's birthday?

2. _____ do they live?

3. _____ does your school start?

4. _____ are your shoes?

B 단어를 바르게 배열하여 문장을 완성하세요.

1. were / born / you / where → _____
   너는 어디에서 태어났니?

2. my / are / where / sunglasses → _____
   내 선글라스는 어디 있니?

3. do / when / go to bed / you → _____
   너는 언제 잠자리에 드니?

4. happy / when / you / are → _____
   너는 언제 행복하니?

5. Hyeri's / is / birthday / when → _____
   혜리의 생일은 언제니?

6. you / do / where / to go / want → _____
   너는 어디에 가고 싶니?

C 다음 질문에 알맞은 대답을 연결하세요.

1. When did you go to the dentist? •   • I usually get up at 6:30.

2. Where do you want to travel? •   • They will go to the lake tomorrow.

3. When do you usually get up? •   • I want to travel to Rome.

4. Where can I find a melon? •   • I went to the dentist a month ago.

5. Where is Tim? •   • He is in the bathroom.

6. When will they go to the lake? •   • You can find one in the fruit section.

Unit 4 how, why

의문사 how는 '어떻게'라는 뜻으로 상태나 방법을 물어볼 때 쓰여요. 또한, how 뒤에 형용사가 오면 '얼마나'라는 뜻으로 다양한 의문문을 만들 수 있어요.

How + 동사 ~?

A: How are you? 어떻게 지내?

A: How do you go to school?
너는 학교에 어떻게 가니?

B: I'm good. 잘 지내.

B: I go to school by bus.
나는 버스를 타고 학교에 가.

How + 형용사 + be동사 + 주어 ~?

A: How old are you? 너는 몇 살이니?

A: How tall is she? 그녀는 키가 얼마나 되니?

A: How much is it? 그거 얼마예요?

B: I'm twelve years old. 나는 열두 살이야.

B: She is 160cm tall. 그녀는 키가 160cm야.

B: It is three dollars. 3달러예요.

의문사 why는 '왜'라는 뜻으로 이유나 원인을 물어볼 때 쓰여요. Why로 질문하면 '왜냐하면'이란 뜻의 Because 로 대답을 시작할 수 있어요.

A: Why are you sad?
너 왜 슬프니?

A: Why do you learn English?
너는 왜 영어를 배우니?

A: Why did he leave early?
그는 왜 일찍 떠났니?

B: (Because) my friend moved to Daejeon.
내 친구가 대전으로 이사갔어.

B: I want to make international friends.
전세계의 친구들을 사귀고 싶어서.

B: He was tired.
피곤해서.

차곡차곡 기초 다지기

우리말 뜻을 읽고 알맞은 의문사에 동그라미 하세요.

1. 너는 어떻게 기타를 칠 수 있니?

   How Why Do you play the guitar?

2. 너는 학교에 왜 늦었니?

   How Why were you late for school?

3. 너는 왜 그렇게 기쁘니?

   How Why are you so happy?

4. 너는 키가 얼마나 되니?

   How Why tall are you?

A 빈칸에 알맞은 형용사를 골라 넣어 문장을 완성하세요.

big   long   deep   far   much

1. How _____ is your hair? 네 머리카락은 얼마나 기니?

2. How _____ is this cap? 이 모자는 얼마예요?

3. How _____ is the river? 그 강은 얼마나 깊나요?

4. How _____ are the dinosaurs? 그 공룡들은 얼마나 큰가요?

5. How _____ is the museum? 그 박물관은 얼마나 머나요?

B 다음 문장에서 <u>틀린</u> 부분을 찾아 바르게 고쳐 쓰세요.

1. How are you crying?   ➡ _____
   너는 왜 울고 있니?

2. Why are she upset?   ➡ _____
   그녀는 왜 기분이 안 좋니?

3. What do you like spring?   ➡ _____
   너는 왜 봄을 좋아하니?

4. Why did he studies history?   ➡ _____
   그는 왜 역사를 공부했니?

C 다음 질문에 알맞은 대답을 연결하세요.

1. How is she?   •   • He has a project to finish.

2. Why do you want to take a taxi?   •   • Because my bag is very heavy.

3. Why is he busy?   •   • Because it is my birthday today.

4. How often do you play outside?   •   • He is ten years old.

5. How old is your brother?   •   • I play outside every day.

6. Why are you happy?   •   • She is fine.

1. 다음 중 의문사에 대한 설명으로 **틀린** 것을 고르세요.

   ① what은 '무엇'이라는 뜻이다.
   ② which는 정해진 범위에서 어떤 것에 대해 물어볼 때 사용한다.
   ③ who는 '누구'인지 물어볼 때 사용한다.
   ④ whose는 '누구의 것'인지 물어볼 때 사용한다.
   ⑤ Who, Whose로 시작하는 의문문에는 Yes나 No로 대답한다.

2. 다음 중 의문사에 대한 설명으로 바른 것을 고르세요.

   ① where는 시간을 물어볼 때 사용한다.
   ② when은 이유를 물어볼 때 사용한다.
   ③ how 뒤에 형용사를 붙여서 질문할 수 있다.
   ④ why 뒤에 형용사를 붙여서 질문할 수 있다.
   ⑤ 방법을 물을 때는 why, 이유를 물을 때는 how 를 쓴다.

3. 다음 중 의문사가 쓰이지 **않은** 문장을 고르세요.

   ① Will you come to the meeting?
   ② Whose dog is this?
   ③ What is your name?
   ④ Which shirt do you like better, this one or that one?
   ⑤ Why were you late today?

[4~7] 빈칸에 알맞은 의문사를 고르세요.

4. _____ much is this cup?

   이 컵은 얼마예요?
   ① Why   ② Where
   ③ How   ④ Who
   ⑤ What

5. _____ is the lady at the front door?

   정문에 계신 여자분은 누구신가요?
   ① Whose   ② Who
   ③ Where   ④ Why
   ⑤ Which

6. _____ do you go to school?

   너는 어떻게 학교에 가니?
   ① When   ② Where
   ③ Who   ④ How
   ⑤ Why

7. _____ hat do you want to buy, the white one or the black one?

   너는 어떤 모자를 사고 싶니, 흰색 아니면 검정색?
   ① What   ② Which
   ③ Whose   ④ Why
   ⑤ How

[8~13] 단어를 바르게 배열하여 문장을 완성하세요.

8. | color | your | What | hair | is |

   ➜ _____

9. | it | cellphone | is | Whose |

   ➜ _____

10. | you | When | come | will |

    ➜ _____

11. your is Where father

➜ _____

12. Why so are happy they

➜ _____

13. heavy the backpack How is

➜ _____

[14~17] 다음 보기 중 질문에 알맞은 대답을 고르세요.

① It's Jeff's.
② It is tomorrow.
③ Because it is fun.
④ I'm playing with my dog.

14. A: What are you doing?
B: (　　　)

15. A: Why do you like drawing?
B: (　　　)

16. A: When is the next game?
B: (　　　)

17. A: Whose cup is it?
B: (　　　)

[18~21] 다음 문장에서 **틀린** 부분을 찾아 바르게 고쳐 쓰세요.

18. How is long this snake?
이 뱀은 얼마나 기니?

➜ _____

19. Whose is faster, a boat or a bicycle?
배와 자전거 중 어떤 것이 더 빠르니?

➜ _____

20. When is your lunch box?
너의 도시락은 어디 있어?

➜ _____

21. How size is this shirt?
이 셔츠는 무슨 사이즈야?

➜ _____

[22~25] 빈칸에 알맞은 단어를 골라 넣어 글을 완성하세요.

Where   How   What   Why

Jenny went to Australia last summer. She made many Australian friends. They asked her many questions. "²² _____ is your name?" "²³ _____ old are you?" "²⁴ _____ did you come to Australia?" "²⁵ _____ is South Korea?" Jenny was excited to meet new friends.

일반동사 현재형	일반동사 과거형	일반동사 현재형	일반동사 과거형
go 가다	went	sell 팔다	sold
write 쓰다	wrote	think 생각하다	thought
swim 수영하다	swam	take 데리고 가다	took
sit 앉다	sat	leave 떠나다	left
have 가지고 있다	had	run 달리다	ran
make 만들다	made	feed 먹이를 주다	fed
do 하다	did	sleep 자다	slept
win 이기다	won	throw 던지다	threw
feel 느끼다	felt	rise 오르다	rose
read 읽다	read	say 말하다	said
find 찾다	found	know 알다	knew
speak 말하다	spoke	buy 사다	bought
drink 마시다	drank	come 오다	came
see 보다	saw	draw 그리다	drew
eat 먹다	ate	cut 자르다	cut
sing 노래하다	sang	fall 떨어지다	fell
put 놓다	put	get 얻다	got
drive 운전하다	drove	fly 날다	flew
hear 듣다	heard	lose 잃어버리다	lost
give 주다	gave	tell 말하다	told
meet 만나다	met	begin 시작하다	began
teach 가르치다	taught	forget 잊어버리다	forgot

▶ **다음 동사의 과거형을 쓰세요.**

일반동사 **현재형**	일반동사 **과거형**	일반동사 **현재형**	일반동사 **과거형**
go 가다		sell 팔다	
write 쓰다		think 생각하다	
swim 수영하다		take 데리고 가다	
sit 앉다		leave 떠나다	
have 가지고 있다		run 달리다	
make 만들다		feed 먹이를 주다	
do 하다		sleep 자다	
win 이기다		throw 던지다	
feel 느끼다		rise 오르다	
read 읽다		say 말하다	
find 찾다		know 알다	
speak 말하다		buy 사다	
drink 마시다		come 오다	
see 보다		draw 그리다	
eat 먹다		cut 자르다	
sing 노래하다		fall 떨어지다	
put 놓다		get 얻다	
drive 운전하다		fly 날다	
hear 듣다		lose 잃어버리다	
give 주다		tell 말하다	
meet 만나다		begin 시작하다	
teach 가르치다		forget 잊어버리다	

정답

Chapter 01 영어 문장 이해하기

Unit 1 단어, 구, 문장

차곡차곡 기초 다지기 ················· p.12

1. 단어   2. 구   3. 문장
4. 단어   5. 문장   6. 구
7. 단어   8. 문장   9. 구
10. 구   11. 단어   12. 구

으쌰으쌰 실력 키우기 ················· p.13

Ⓐ 1. 단어   2. 없다   3. 나타내는   4. 대문자
Ⓑ 1. in   2. scary   3. iced
   4. small   5. seven   6. favorite
Ⓒ 1. students   2. has
   3. sing and dance   4. in trees

Unit 2 8품사

차곡차곡 기초 다지기 ················· p.14

1. 대명사   2. 명사   3. 형용사
4. 전치사   5. 전치사   6. 부사
7. 명사   8. 명사   9. 감탄사
10. 접속사   11. 동사   12. 접속사

으쌰으쌰 실력 키우기 ················· p.15

Ⓐ 1. and   2. very   3. jump
   4. She   5. smart   6. on
   7. Ouch   8. desk
Ⓑ 1. friend   2. hot   3. in
   4. Wow   5. so   6. writes
Ⓒ 1. 동사, 부사   2. 대명사, 전치사, 명사
   3. 동사, 형용사, 접속사   4. 감탄사, 형용사, 명사

Unit 3 문장의 종류

차곡차곡 기초 다지기 ················· p.16

1. 의문문   2. 평서문   3. 감탄문   4. 명령문

으쌰으쌰 실력 키우기 ················· p.17

Ⓐ 1. 평서문   2. 감탄문   3. 의문문   4. 명령문
Ⓑ 1. My name is Jade.
   2. How sad it is!
   3. Close the door.
   4. Do you like bananas?
Ⓒ 1. What   2. How   3. is   4. Stand

꼼꼼하게 종합평가 p.18~19

1. ④   2. ②   3. ①   4. ⑤   5. ②
6. ①   7. ③   8. ②   9. ④   10. ②
11. 의문문   12. 감탄문   13. 평서문   14. 명령문
15. ②   16. flowers   17. a student
18. brown   19. at the library
20. My brother and I like cheese pizza.
21. Do you walk to school?
22. She is at the store.
23. 명사   24. 부사   25. 형용사

[23~25]

해석 안녕, 나는 민호야. 나는 영어를 좋아해. 그것은 재미있어. 나는 뉴욕에서 온 친구가 있어. 그녀의 이름은 제니야. 제니는 매우 친절해. 얼마나 좋은 친구인지 몰라!

Chapter 02 명사와 관사

Unit 1 셀 수 있는 명사

차곡차곡 기초 다지기 ················· p.22

book, clock, chair, desk, student, teacher

으쌰으쌰 실력 키우기 ················· p.23

Ⓐ 1. buses   2. benches   3. men
   4. potatoes   5. leaves   6. chairs
   7. teeth   8. babies
Ⓑ 1. cars   2. fish   3. foxes
   4. pencils   5. ladies   6. mice
   7. knives   8. dishes

C 1. dogs 　　　　　 2. strawberries
　　3. tomatoes 　　　 4. children
　　5. boxes 　　　　　 6. feet

Unit 2 셀 수 없는 명사

차곡차곡 **기초** 다지기 ·························· p.24

1. 추상명사 　　　 2. 물질명사 　　　 3. 추상명사
4. 고유명사 　　　 5. 물질명사 　　　 6. 고유명사
7. 추상명사 　　　 8. 물질명사

으쌰으쌰 **실력** 키우기 ·························· p.25

A 셀 수 있는 명사: brother, fish, woman, crayon,
　　　　　　　　　 knife, pig, orange
　　셀 수 없는 명사: Paris, butter, juice, salt, love
B 1. cup 　　　　 2. bag 　　　　 3. pieces
　　4. loaves 　　 5. glass 　　　 6. slices
C 1. a Daniel → This is Daniel.
　　2. musics → I love music.
　　3. march → My birthday is in March.
　　4. milks → We drink two cups of milk.
　　5. spain → He is from Spain.

Unit 3 부정관사 a/an

차곡차곡 **기초** 다지기 ·························· p.26

a onion, a airplane, an kite, an mail,
a owl, a eraser

으쌰으쌰 **실력** 키우기 ·························· p.27

A 1. a 　　　　 2. an 　　　　 3. ✕
　　4. ✕ 　　　　 5. an 　　　　 6. an
　　7. a 　　　　 8. ✕ 　　　　 9. a
B 1. a 　　　　 2. an 　　　　 3. a
　　4. an 　　　　 5. an
C 1. An octopus has eight legs.
　　2. My grandmother is a good cook.
　　3. A turtle is slow.
　　4. I have an umbrella.

Unit 4 정관사 the

차곡차곡 **기초** 다지기 ·························· p.28

1. play the cello 　　　 2. in the sky
3. study math 　　　　 4. have dinner
5. play tennis 　　　　 6. speak English
7. on the moon 　　　 8. play the violin

으쌰으쌰 **실력** 키우기 ·························· p.29

A 1. the 　　 2. 붙인다 　　 3. the 　　 4. 이미 언급한
B 1. ✕ 　　 2. The 　　 3. ✕ 　　 4. The 　　 5. the
C 1. the table 　　　　 2. the sky
　　3. the guitar 　　　　 4. The elephant

꼼꼼하게 **종합평가** p.30~31

1. ② 　　 2. ④ 　　 3. ⑤ 　　 4. ④ 　　 5. ②
6. ⑤ 　　 7. ② 　　 8. a 　　 9. the 　　 10. A
11. the 　 12. an 　 13. ① 　 14. ④ 　 15. ①
16. geese 　　 17. candies 　　 18. cars
19. I need a piece of paper.
20. I see five monkeys.
21. Love is great.
22. I drink a glass of water.
23. a 　　　　 24. the 　　　　 25. an

[23~25]
해석 제니는 학생이다. 그녀는 음악을 좋아한다. 그녀는 하모니카를 분다. 하모니카 소리는 아름답다. 그녀는 매일 오렌지 먹는 것을 좋아한다. 그것은 그녀가 제일 좋아하는 과일이다.

Chapter 03 대명사

Unit 1 주격 인칭대명사

차곡차곡 **기초** 다지기 ·························· p.34

she: 그녀는 　　　 he: 그는 　　　 you(복수): 너희들은
they: 그(것)들은 　 I: 나는 　　　　 it: 그것은
you(단수): 너는 　 we: 우리는

으쌰으쌰 **실력** 키우기 ·· p.35

Ⓐ 1. she   2. you   3. he
    4. they   5. we   6. it
    7. they   8. he

Ⓑ 1. I   2. They   3. You
    4. She   5. We

Ⓒ 1. Junho → He   2. Cats → They
    3. The camera → It   4. John and I → We
    5. The boys and girls → They

Unit 2   소유격 인칭대명사

차곡차곡 **기초** 다지기 ·· p.36

1. my   2. our   3. their   4. his
5. its   6. your   7. her

으쌰으쌰 **실력** 키우기 ·· p.37

Ⓐ 1. its   2. her   3. your
    4. my   5. our   6. their
    7. your   8. his

Ⓑ 1. ⓨour milk is on the table.
    2. Mr. Son is Ⓞur teacher.
    3. Ⓗis box is heavy.
    4. Amy and John ride Ⓣheir horses.

Ⓒ 1. its   2. your   3. My
    4. our   5. Her

Unit 3   목적격 인칭대명사

차곡차곡 **기초** 다지기 ·· p.38

them: 그(것)들을   her: 그녀를
you(단수): 너를   him: 그를
us: 우리를   you(복수): 너희들을
it: 그것을   me: 나를

으쌰으쌰 **실력** 키우기 ·· p.39

Ⓐ 1. you   2. us   3. him   4. her
    5. it   6. them   7. me   8. you

Ⓑ 1. it   2. us   3. him   4. you

Ⓒ 1. ②   2. ④   3. ③   4. ①

Unit 4   소유대명사

차곡차곡 **기초** 다지기 ·· p.40

ours: 우리의 것   hers: 그녀의 것
yours(단수): 너의 것   theirs: 그들의 것
his: 그의 것   mine: 나의 것
yours(복수): 너희들의 것

으쌰으쌰 **실력** 키우기 ·· p.41

Ⓐ 1. mine   2. theirs   3. hers   4. his
    5. yours   6. yours   7. ours

Ⓑ 1. theirs   2. Ours   3. his
    4. Hers   5. Yours

Ⓒ 1. yours   2. his   3. mine
    4. ours   5. Theirs

Unit 5   지시대명사

차곡차곡 **기초** 다지기 ·· p.42

that: 저것   this: 이것
those: 저것들   these: 이것들
this cookie: 이 쿠키   those chairs: 저 의자들
these trucks: 이 트럭들   that store: 저 가게

으쌰으쌰 **실력** 키우기 ·· p.43

Ⓐ 1. this   2. those   3. that   4. these

Ⓑ 1. Ⓣhat is a desk.
    2. Ⓣhis is my mother.
    3. Ⓣhese are soccer balls.
    4. Ⓣhose are Sumi's parents.

Ⓒ 1. These firefighters   2. That flower
    3. Those babies   4. This present

Unit 6   비인칭주어 it

차곡차곡 **기초** 다지기 ·· p.44

sunny, Friday, near, 10:30, cool, May 31, winter

으쌰으쌰 **실력** 키우기 ·· p.45

Ⓐ 1. 인칭대명사 it   2. 비인칭주어 it
    3. 인칭대명사 it   4. 비인칭주어 it
    5. 비인칭주어 it   6. 인칭대명사 it

B 1. It is August 15.

2. It is warm.

3. It is 10 meters.

4. It is summer.

5. It is one fifteen.

C 1. cloudy 2. Monday

3. December 18 4. nine o'clock

🛥 **꼼꼼하게 종합평가** p.46~47

1. ⑤ 2. ② 3. ④ 4. ① 5. ③
6. ⑤ 7. ④ 8. ② 9. ⑤ 10. ④
11. ③ 12. ③ 13. That 14. It
15. She 16. yours
17. she, my 18. these, eggs
19. The house is theirs.
20. Jimmy likes it.
21. His bag is heavy.
22. His 23. He 24. him 25. his

[22~25]

해석 제니는 남동생이 있다. 그의 이름은 라이언이다. 그는 7살이다. 제니는 그와 함께 논다. 라이언은 축구공을 가지고 있다. 그것은 그의 것이다.

Chapter 04 be동사

Unit 1 be동사 am, are, is

차곡차곡 **기초** 다지기 p.50

We, You, They: are I: am He, She, It: is

으쌰으쌰 **실력** 키우기 p.51

A 1. are 2. are 3. is
4. is 5. am 6. is

B 1. is 2. are 3. is
4. am 5. is 6. are

C 1. It is a bird.

2. My sisters are in Florida.

3. I am a pilot.

4. Julia is kind.

Unit 2 be동사 긍정문과 부정문

차곡차곡 **기초** 다지기 p.52

They, You, We: are not
She, It, He: is not I: am not

으쌰으쌰 **실력** 키우기 p.53

A 1. are 2. isn't 3. is
4. am not 5. isn't 6. are

B 1. We are not (= aren't) in France.

2. They are chocolate cookies.

3. I am not cold.

4. It is difficult.

C 1. My sister is sick.

2. You aren't a singer.

3. The backpack isn't on the desk.

4. I am busy.

Unit 3 be동사 의문문

차곡차곡 **기초** 다지기 p.54

1. Am I 2. Is he 3. Are you
4. Is it 5. Are we 6. Are they

으쌰으쌰 **실력** 키우기 p.55

A 1. Are they 2. Are you
3. Is she 4. Is it
5. Are they 6. Is he

B 1. Are you a soccer player?

2. Is the movie boring?

3. Are they gorillas?

4. Is John a good boy?

C 1. you, not 2. Is, he
3. Are, Yes 4. it, isn't

🛥 **꼼꼼하게 종합평가** p.56~57

1. ④ 2. ④ 3. ② 4. ③ 5. ②
6. Are 7. isn't 8. are 9. am 10. Is
11. ② 12. ④ 13. ③ 14. ①
15. He is angry.
16. Are the birds on the tree?

17. You aren't ugly.
18. She is not sick.
19. Is the book boring?
20. are, No 　　　21. Is, it
22. is 　　23. are 　　24. is 　　25. isn't

[22~25]

해석 오늘은 제니의 생일이다. 그녀의 조부모님은 제니의 집에 계신다. 생일 케이크는 식탁 위에 놓여 있다. 그녀는 11살일까? 그렇지 않다. 그녀는 12살이다.

Chapter 05 일반동사

Unit 1 일반동사 현재형

차곡차곡 기초 다지기 ················· p.60

eat, sleep, walk, smile, study, play, talk

으쌰으쌰 실력 키우기 ················· p.61

Ⓐ 1. draws 　　2. listen 　　3. drink
　　4. move 　　5. waters 　　6. bake
Ⓑ 1. washes 　　2. meets 　　3. travels
　　4. studies 　　5. goes 　　6. has
Ⓒ 1. Bees make honey.
　　2. Mary has a little lamb.
　　3. My mom drinks coffee.
　　4. Derek watches a movie.

Unit 2 일반동사 부정문

차곡차곡 기초 다지기 ················· p.62

We, Her friends, I, They, Jay and I: don't
He, The lady, A donut, The dog, Samuel, She, It: doesn't

으쌰으쌰 실력 키우기 ················· p.63

Ⓐ 1. doesn't 　　　　2. don't
　　3. does not 　　　4. do not
Ⓑ 1. I know her name.
　　2. Suyeon doesn't buy toys.
　　3. The girls jump on the bed.
　　4. The train doesn't stop at the station.

Ⓒ 1. She doesn't teach math.
　　2. We don't speak loudly.
　　3. The grasshopper doesn't work.
　　4. The boy doesn't look good.

Unit 3 일반동사 의문문

차곡차곡 기초 다지기 ················· p.64

1. Does he have 　　2. Does it start
3. Do you drive 　　4. Does the man fix
5. Do they carry 　　6. Do the kids play

으쌰으쌰 실력 키우기 ················· p.65

Ⓐ 1. Does the bakery make cakes?
　　2. Do you swim in the morning?
　　3. Does the sun set in the evening?
　　4. Does the giraffe eat grass?
Ⓑ 1. Do you speak English?
　　2. Do they trust him?
　　3. Does he have a sore throat?
　　4. Do the fruits smell good?
Ⓒ 1. Do, don't 　　　2. he, does
　　3. they, Yes 　　　4. she, doesn't

꼼꼼하게 종합평가 p.66~67

1. ② 　　　2. ④ 　　　3. ② 　　　4. ⑤
5. The class doesn't finish at 12.
6. They don't wear uniforms.
7. Jake doesn't live in Korea.
8. Do you like the story?
9. Does a doctor help sick people?
10. Do your friends like swimming?
11. ① 　　12. ③ 　　13. ② 　　14. ④
15. I finish my homework in the evening.
16. The farmer feeds the animals.
17. Lemons don't taste sweet.
18. We dance at the party.
19. Sally rides a bicycle.
20. Do, Yes 　　　21. Does, doesn't
22. bakes 　　　23. helps
24. doesn't 　　　25. Does

^{해석} 제니의 할머니가 제니와 그녀의 남동생을 위해 쿠키를 굽는다. 제니는 할머니를 도와드린다. 제니의 남동생은 할머니를 도와드리지 않는다. 그러나 그는 얼마 후 쿠키를 먹는다. 제니의 할머니가 그를 좋아할까? 할머니는 물론 그를 좋아한다.

Chapter 6 시제

Unit 1 현재진행형

차곡차곡 기초 다지기 p.70

1. driving   2. reading   3. stopping
4. coming   5. washing   6. swimming

으쌰으쌰 실력 키우기 p.71

Ⓐ 1. am writing   2. is talking
   3. are baking   4. are singing
Ⓑ 1. They are not (= aren't) watching a movie.
   2. The boy is not (= isn't) doing his homework.
   3. I am not traveling to New York.
   4. They are not (= aren't) kicking balls.
Ⓒ 1. No, it isn't.   2. No, she isn't.
   3. Yes, I am.   4. Yes, they are.

Unit 2 be동사 과거형

차곡차곡 기초 다지기 p.72

1. was, wasn't   2. were, weren't
3. was, wasn't   4. were, weren't
5. were, weren't   6. was, wasn't
7. was, wasn't   8. was, wasn't

으쌰으쌰 실력 키우기 p.73

Ⓐ 1. was   2. were   3. was   4. were
   5. was   6. was   7. were   8. was
Ⓑ 1. She was not (= wasn't) hungry.
   2. Was he a soccer player?
   3. They were not (= weren't) nice.
   4. Was the trip fun?
Ⓒ 1. I was   2. No, it
   3. wasn't, was   4. Yes, were

Unit 3 일반동사 과거형

차곡차곡 기초 다지기 p.74

1. worked   2. wrote   3. went
4. cried   5. used   6. stopped

으쌰으쌰 실력 키우기 p.75

Ⓐ 1. study → studied   2. plays → played
   3. eat → ate   4. orders → ordered
   5. see → saw   6. read → read
Ⓑ 1. smiled   2. shared
   3. ran   4. asked
Ⓒ 1. Jim dropped the vase.
   2. They traveled to Mexico.
   3. Amy cleaned the room.
   4. He felt sick.

Unit 4 일반동사 과거형 부정문과 의문문

차곡차곡 기초 다지기 p.76

1. ○   2. ✕   3. ✕   4. ○
5. ✕   6. ○   7. ○   8. ✕

으쌰으쌰 실력 키우기 p.77

Ⓐ 1. didn't brush   2. didn't try
   3. didn't clean   4. didn't know
Ⓑ 1. Did the dog play with a ball?
   2. Did Grandpa sit on the bench?
   3. Did the horse run a race?
   4. Did it snow yesterday?
Ⓒ 1. No, didn't   2. finish, did
   3. Did, he   4. make, Yes

Unit 5 동사의 미래형 (will, be going to)

차곡차곡 기초 다지기 p.78

1. I will write a letter.
2. Will Steve make lunch?
3. Tom will not run.
4. We are going to play.

오쌰오쌰 **실력** 키우기 ·· p.79

Ⓐ 1. not　　2. swim　　3. Will　　4. play
Ⓑ 1. We will not (= won't) exercise.
　　2. Will Loren return the book?
　　3. I will not (= won't) finish my work.
　　4. Will Grandmother visit us?
Ⓒ 1. Will, I　　　　　　2. go, won't
　　3. help, Yes　　　　4. play, No

꼼꼼하게 **종합평가** p.80~81

1. ②　　2. ⑤　　3. ④　　4. ③
5. Noah is writing a card.
6. Will you go to the park?
7. They were hot.
8. We didn't read the book.
9. She slept on the sofa.
10. It is going to rain.
11. ④　　12. ②　　13. ③　　14. ①
15. We are jumping on the bed.
16. The girl didn't close the door.
17. The children were not hungry.
18. We will promise you.
19. He is working at the office.
20. Are, Yes, having
21. ride, didn't, played
22. met　　23. were　　24. didn't　　25. go

[22~25]
해석 제니는 수지를 만났다. 그들은 해변에 있었다. 그들은 수영을 하지 않았다. 그들은 모래성을 만들었다. 그들은 즐거운 시간을 보냈다. 그들은 언젠가 다시 해변에 갈 것이다.

Chapter 07 형용사와 부사

Unit 1 형용사의 의미와 쓰임

차곡차곡 **기초** 다지기 ·· p.84

1. car　　2. weather　3. game　　4. candy
5. test　　6. book　　7. eye　　8. apple

오쌰오쌰 **실력** 키우기 ·· p.85

Ⓐ 1. red　2. slow　3. big　4. old　5. ten
Ⓑ 1. She has a (round) face.
　　2. It is a (lovely) picture.
　　3. The rabbit is (soft).
　　4. The teacher is (kind).
　　5. David is (brave).
　　6. He has (short) hair.
Ⓒ 1. 1) hot　　2) tall　　　3) long
　　2. 1) deep　　2) fast　　　3) sharp

Unit 2 수량형용사

차곡차곡 **기초** 다지기 ·· p.86

1. ✕　　2. ○　　3. ○　　4. ✕
5. ○　　6. ○　　7. ○　　8. ✕

오쌰오쌰 **실력** 키우기 ·· p.87

Ⓐ 1. Many　2. much　3. much　4. Many
Ⓑ 1. All　　2. all　　3. every　4. every
Ⓒ 1. some　2. any　　3. some　4. any

Unit 3 부사의 의미와 쓰임

차곡차곡 **기초** 다지기 ·· p.88

really, early, very, happily, softly, carefully, now, clearly

오쌰오쌰 **실력** 키우기 ·· p.89

Ⓐ 1. really　　　2. sadly　　　3. slowly
　　4. carefully　　5. so　　　　6. early
Ⓑ 1. The little duck is so cute.
　　2. Ellen did her work well.
　　3. The girls answered politely.
　　4. My teacher talks too fast.
　　5. I finished the homework finally.
　　6. It is very cold in Alaska.
Ⓒ 1. bright　　2. really　　3. too
　　4. now　　　5. happily　　6. hard

Unit 4 빈도부사

차곡차곡 **기초** 다지기 ············· p.90

1. usually
2. sometimes
3. never
4. rarely
5. always
6. often

으쌰으쌰 **실력** 키우기 ············· p.91

Ⓐ
1. never
2. often
3. always
4. usually
5. rarely
6. sometimes

Ⓑ
1. Becky sometimes watches a movie.
2. My parents are always patient.
3. I usually finish my homework.
4. He will never buy toys.
5. It rarely snows in Texas.
6. He is often late for school.

Ⓒ
1. He is always nice.
2. She often reads books.
3. I will never forget you.
4. They sometimes play tennis.

꼼꼼하게 종합평가 p.92~93

1. ②, ④
2. ⑤
3. ②
4. ③
5. ②
6. ④
7. ②
8. ⑤
9. The elephant is huge.
10. I don't have any milk.
11. You are really wonderful.
12. We always study English.
13. ③
14. ④
15. ②
16. ③
17. My uncle has brown hair.
18. I exercise every day.
19. The woman often buys fresh eggs.
20. too, really
21. any, some
22. alone
23. sometimes
24. writes
25. very

[22~25]

해석 제니는 그녀의 방에 혼자 있다. 그녀는 가끔 조용한 시간을 갖는다. 그녀는 보통 일기를 쓴다. 그녀는 글 쓰는 것을 매우 좋아한다.

Chapter 08 비교급과 전치사

Unit 1 비교급

차곡차곡 **기초** 다지기 ············· p.96

1. colder
2. shorter
3. hotter
4. softer
5. prettier
6. larger

으쌰으쌰 **실력** 키우기 ············· p.97

Ⓐ
1. cleaner
2. worse
3. longer
4. more exciting
5. heavier
6. more difficult
7. nicer
8. bigger

Ⓑ
1. younger
2. wiser
3. more powerful
4. sweeter
5. cheaper
6. slower

Ⓒ
1. She is busier than me.
2. A giraffe is taller than an elephant.
3. I am faster than you.
4. Apples are bigger than cherries.
5. English is more interesting than math.

Unit 2 최상급

차곡차곡 **기초** 다지기 ············· p.98

best, coldest, largest, worst, biggest, easiest

으쌰으쌰 **실력** 키우기 ············· p.99

Ⓐ
1. sweetest
2. longest
3. busiest
4. hottest
5. thickest
6. most difficult
7. happiest
8. most important

Ⓑ
1. the largest
2. the highest
3. the most dangerous
4. the most popular

Ⓒ
1. It is the biggest star in the sky.
2. I am the fastest in my class.
3. It is the most beautiful day in my life.

Unit 3 시간 전치사

차곡차곡 **기초** 다지기 ······································ p.100

1. in   2. after   3. before
4. on   5. in   6. at

으쌰으쌰 **실력** 키우기 ······································ p.101

Ⓐ 1. in   2. on   3. on
   4. at   5. on   6. in
Ⓑ 1. at   2. in   3. after
   4. on   5. before
Ⓒ 1. for   2. before   3. on
   4. in   5. after   6. on

Unit 4 장소/방향 전치사

차곡차곡 **기초** 다지기 ······································ p.102

1. under   2. next to   3. on
4. in front of   5. in   6. behind
7. to   8. from

으쌰으쌰 **실력** 키우기 ······································ p.103

Ⓐ 1. under   2. in   3. behind
   4. next to   5. to   6. in front of
   7. on   8. from
Ⓑ 1. Your key is on the table.
   2. Erin sits next to Doyoung.
   3. The cat is hiding behind the box.
   4. They are swimming in the pool.
Ⓒ 1. Miles is from South Africa.
   2. A dog is in front of his house.
   3. The students are walking to the library.
   4. Some flowers are in the vase.

Unit 5 There is, There are

차곡차곡 **기초** 다지기 ······································ p.104

There is: an ant, a pencil, some water, a book, a slide

There are: shoes, ten apples, cherries, ducks, many children

으쌰으쌰 **실력** 키우기 ······································ p.105

Ⓐ 1. There is   2. There are
   3. There is   4. There are
Ⓑ 1. There isn't a bus to the museum.
   2. Are there two children in front of the gate?
   3. There aren't butterflies on the flower.
   4. Is there a candy in the drawer?
Ⓒ 1. Yes, there is.   2. No, there aren't.
   3. No, there isn't. 4. Yes, there are.

꼼꼼하게 종합평가 p.106~107

1. ④   2. ⑤   3. ②   4. ①   5. ②
6. ②   7. ③   8. ③   9. ①   10. ②
11. There are bananas on the tray.
12. They are waiting behind the gate.
13. We have English class on Monday.
14. She is the prettiest girl in town.
15. A ship is bigger than a boat.
16. Hope is stronger than fear.
17. My mother is the most beautiful woman in the world.
18. We eat rice cake soup on New Year's Day.
19. Is there a store next to the school?
20. The trip starts on July 23rd.
21. There isn't any bread in the bakery.
22. to   23. in   24. most   25. on

[22~25]

해석 제니는 미국에 갔다. 샌프란시스코에는 다리가 있다. 그것은 미국에서 가장 유명한 다리이다. 그녀는 그 다리 위에서 사진을 찍었다.

Chapter 09 조동사

Unit 1 can

차곡차곡 **기초** 다지기 ······································ p.110

1. write   2. jump   3. see
4. go   5. finish   6. eat
7. drink   8. speak   9. move

Ⓐ 1. They can play tennis.
   2. Spencer can sing songs.
   3. Lewis can write stories.
   4. I can climb the mountain.
Ⓑ 1. Can we watch the cartoon?
   2. Ethan can't drive a car.
   3. Can you clean your room?
   4. Denise can't ride a horse.
Ⓒ 1. Can, Yes, I   2. you, can't
   3. he, can   4. No, can't

Unit 2 may

listen, begin, come, open, visit, have

Ⓐ 1. The dog may eat bones.
   2. You may play in the water.
   3. Hanna may go to the concert.
   4. Ron may play soccer.
   5. They may open the box.
   6. He may bake cookies.
Ⓑ 1. May I sit here?
   2. They may not use this door.
   3. May I help you?
   4. Visitors may not feed the animals.
Ⓒ 1. May I join you?
   2. You may not run in the hallways.
   3. May we watch television?
   4. May I wear boots?

Unit 3 must, should

1. watch   2. take   3. be
4. sleep   5. clean   6. play
7. say   8. drink   9. cook

Ⓐ 1. must be   2. should talk
   3. have to find   4. should read

5. must not take
Ⓑ 1. I should not finish my homework.
   2. They must not drink milk.
   3. She should not stay home today.
   4. I don't have to sleep on the sofa.
Ⓒ 1. They should try bibimbap.
   2. You must not tell a lie.
   3. All students must wear school uniforms.
   4. We should not drive fast.

1. ③   2. ④   3. ①   4. ④   5. ③
6. ③   7. ①   8. ②   9. ③
10. You should exercise regularly.
11. Andy may ride a bicycle.
12. He can't use a computer.
13. Children must wear seat belts.
14. May I come in?
15. You shouldn't eat junk food.
16. ③   17. ⑤
18. Larry can understand me.
19. You should drink more water.
20. They may come to the party.
21. She must practice hard.
22. can dance   23. should wear
24. may not   25. must follow

[22~25]
해석 제니는 발레를 할 수 있다. 그녀는 금요일에 발레 수업이 있다. 그녀는 토 슈즈를 신어야 한다. 그녀는 수업 시간에 떠들면 안 된다. 그녀는 선생님의 지시를 잘 따라야 한다.

Chapter 10 동명사와 to부정사

Unit 1 동명사

1. kicking   2. running   3. going
4. riding   5. meeting   6. winning
7. telling   8. drawing   9. saving

오쌰오쌰 **실력** 키우기 ⋯⋯⋯⋯⋯⋯⋯⋯⋯ p.121

Ⓐ **1.** traveling: 여행하는 것
　　2. Eating: 먹는 것
　　3. listening: 듣는 것
　　4. Studying: 공부하는 것

Ⓑ **1.** 목적어　　**2.** 보어　　**3.** 주어
　　4. 목적어　　**5.** 주어　　**6.** 보어

Ⓒ **1.** reading　　　　　**2.** writing
　　3. collecting　　　　**4.** Making

Unit 2 to부정사

차곡차곡 **기초** 다지기 ⋯⋯⋯⋯⋯⋯⋯⋯⋯ p.122

1. run　　　**2.** ask　　　**3.** take
4. go　　　**5.** see　　　**6.** swim

오쌰오쌰 **실력** 키우기 ⋯⋯⋯⋯⋯⋯⋯⋯⋯ p.123

Ⓐ **1.** I studied hard to pass the exam.

　　2. Sally has snacks to eat.

　　3. We are glad to see you.

　　4. I need crayons to draw.

　　5. This book is fun to read.

　　6. He came to see us.

Ⓑ **1.** 형용사　　**2.** 부사　　**3.** 명사
　　4. 부사　　　**5.** 형용사　**6.** 명사

Ⓒ **1.** to run　　**2.** to eat　　**3.** to ride
　　4. To say　　**5.** to meet　　**6.** to write

꼼꼼하게 **종합평가** p.124~125

1. ①　**2.** ③　**3.** ④　**4.** ③　**5.** ③
6. ①　**7.** ②　**8.** ④　**9.** ③　**10.** ①
11. ④　**12.** ④　**13.** ②

14. The children started to play baseball.
15. Reading English newspaper is interesting.
16. She likes to play the guitar.
17. The farmer has many apples to sell.
18. Playing chess is fun.
19. We enjoy swimming in summer.
20. I have a book to read.
21. The boy likes to collect coins.
22. to draw　　　**23.** enjoys
24. to use　　　　**25.** working

[22~25]

해석 제니는 미술 시간을 좋아한다. 그녀는 꽃을 그리는 것을 좋아한다. 그녀는 채색하는 것을 즐긴다. 그녀는 사용할 새 물감들이 있다. 그녀는 그림 그리는 것을 매우 좋아한다.

Chapter 11 접속사와 명령문

Unit 1 접속사

차곡차곡 **기초** 다지기 ⋯⋯⋯⋯⋯⋯⋯⋯⋯ p.128

1. because　**2.** or　**3.** but　**4.** and　**5.** so

오쌰오쌰 **실력** 키우기 ⋯⋯⋯⋯⋯⋯⋯⋯⋯ p.129

Ⓐ **1.** or　　　　**2.** and　　　**3.** so
　　4. but　　　**5.** because
Ⓑ **1.** but　　　**2.** because　**3.** so
　　4. or　　　**5.** and

Ⓒ **1.** I want a burger and French fries.
　　2. It is cold, so I will wear a warm coat.
　　3. Do you go to school by bus or on foot?
　　4. Jin passed the test because she studied hard.

Unit 2 일반동사 명령문

차곡차곡 **기초** 다지기 ⋯⋯⋯⋯⋯⋯⋯⋯⋯ p.130

Don't talk too fast.
Go to bed.
Do not take pictures in the museum.
Wash your hands.
Close the window, please.

오쌰오쌰 **실력** 키우기 ⋯⋯⋯⋯⋯⋯⋯⋯⋯ p.131

Ⓐ **1.** cry　**2.** Look　**3.** come　**4.** Call　**5.** Wash
Ⓑ **1.** Listen to me.

2. Have a seat, please.
3. Do not use plastic bags.
4. Brush your teeth.
5. Don't forget your homework.

ⓒ 1. ③   2. ④   3. ②   4. ①

Unit 3 be동사 명령문

차곡차곡 기초 다지기 ··· p.132

Be kind.   Don't be scared.
Be quiet, please.   Please don't be angry.
Be honest.

으쌰으쌰 실력 키우기 ··· p.133

Ⓐ 1. Be friendly.
   2. Don't be nervous.
   3. Don't be shy.
   4. Please be polite.
   5. Don't be silly.
   6. Be ready.
Ⓑ 1. Be patient, please.
   2. Don't be upset.
   3. Be careful.
   4. Don't be rude.
   5. Be kind to people.
ⓒ 1. ②   2. ①   3. ③   4. ④

꼼꼼하게 종합평가 p.134~135

1. ⑤   2. ③   3. ②   4. ④   5. ⑤
6. ②   7. ③   8. ①   9. ④   10. ②
11. We finished dinner and ate ice cream.
12. Don't worry.   13. Do your best.
14. Is it a tiger or a lion?
15. Be honest to yourself.
16. I was cold, so I wore a jacket.
17. I like my dog because it's lovely.
18. They are my neighbors, but I don't know them well.
19. Listen carefully, please.
20. Don't be rude.
21. Don't forget me.
22. and   23. Turn   24. Put   25. Wait

[22~25]
해석 제니는 어제 피자를 구웠다. 그것은 쉽고 재미있었다. 요리법은 다음과 같다. 오븐을 켜라. 피자를 오븐 안에 넣어라. 15분 동안 기다려라. 제니는 그녀의 남동생과 그 피자를 나눠 먹었다.

Chapter 12 의문사

Unit 1 what, which

차곡차곡 기초 다지기 ··· p.138

1. What   2. Which   3. What   4. Which

으쌰으쌰 실력 키우기 ··· p.139

Ⓐ 1. What   2. Which
   3. Which   4. What
Ⓑ 1. color   2. backpack
   3. time   4. sport
ⓒ 1. I'm doing my homework.
   2. The red hat is mine.
   3. I like this book.
   4. My hobby is riding a bicycle.
   5. Today is Thursday.
   6. A chair is heavier.

Unit 2 who, whose

차곡차곡 기초 다지기 ··· p.140

Who is he?
Whose umbrella is this?
Who is your friend?
Whose pen is on the table?

으쌰으쌰 실력 키우기 ··· p.141

Ⓐ 1. Whose   2. Whose
   3. Who   4. Who
Ⓑ 1. Who is Janet?
   2. Whose parents are they?
   3. Who are they?
   4. Who is taking pictures?
   5. Whose crayons are those?
   6. Whose car is it?
ⓒ 1. He is my brother.

2. Amy is playing the guitar.

3. Jay is late.

4. It is Michelle's.

5. It's her idea.

6. Philip is at the office.

Unit 3   when, where

차곡차곡 **기초** 다지기 p.142

When does the movie start?

Where is Mom?

When is the vacation?

Where is your school?

으쌰으쌰 **실력** 키우기 p.143

Ⓐ **1.** When   **2.** Where
　 3. When   **4.** Where

Ⓑ **1.** Where were you born?
　 2. Where are my sunglasses?
　 3. When do you go to bed?
　 4. When are you happy?
　 5. When is Hyeri's birthday?
　 6. Where do you want to go?

Ⓒ **1.** I went to the dentist a month ago.
　 2. I want to travel to Rome.
　 3. I usually get up at 6:30.
　 4. You can find one in the fruit section.
　 5. He is in the bathroom.
　 6. They will go to the lake tomorrow.

Unit 4   how, why

차곡차곡 **기초** 다지기 p.144

1. How   **2.** Why   **3.** Why   **4.** How

으쌰으쌰 **실력** 키우기 p.145

Ⓐ **1.** long   **2.** much   **3.** deep   **4.** big   **5.** far

Ⓑ **1.** Why are you crying?
　 2. Why is she upset?
　 3. Why do you like spring?
　 4. Why did he study history?

Ⓒ **1.** She is fine.
　 2. Because my bag is very heavy.

3. He has a project to finish.

4. I play outside every day.

5. He is ten years old.

6. Because it is my birthday today.

꼼꼼하게 종합평가   p.146~147

1. ⑤   **2.** ③   **3.** ①   **4.** ③

5. ②   **6.** ④   **7.** ②

8. What color is your hair?

9. Whose cellphone is it?

10. When will you come?

11. Where is your father?

12. Why are they so happy?

13. How heavy is the backpack?

14. ④   **15.** ③   **16.** ②   **17.** ①

18. How long is this snake?

19. Which is faster, a boat or a bicycle?

20. Where is your lunch box?

21. What size is this shirt?

22. What   **23.** How   **24.** Why   **25.** Where

[22~25]

해석 제니는 지난 여름에 호주에 갔다. 그녀는 많은 호주 친구들을 사귀었다. 그들은 그녀에게 여러 가지 질문을 했다. "이름이 뭐니?" "몇 살이야?" "호주에는 왜 왔어?" "한국은 어디에 있니?" 제니는 새 친구들을 만나서 기뻤다.

문장 쓰기 노트 정답

Chapter 1 영어 문장 이해하기

Unit 1 단어, 구, 문장 문장 쓰기 노트 p.3

Ⓐ 1. I like my cat.
2. I like my puppy.
3. I like my teacher.
4. It is a yellow bus.
5. It is a brown horse.
6. It is a green tree.
7. He has a soccer ball.
8. She has a cup.
9. He has a book.

Ⓑ 1. 별들은 하늘에 있어.
2. 그들은 학생들이야.
3. 나는 매일 아침을 먹어.

Unit 2 8품사 문장 쓰기 노트 p.4

Ⓐ 1. He is Minho.
2. He is my dad.
3. He is my friend.
4. I like baseball and basketball.
5. I like apples and oranges.
6. I like Jenny and Tim.
7. Flowers are very beautiful.
8. The dog is very cute.
9. The milk is very hot.

Ⓑ 1. 개구리들은 높이 뛰어.
2. 우리는 밤에 자.
3. 그녀는 키가 커.

Unit 3 문장의 종류 문장 쓰기 노트 p.5

Ⓐ 1. We are hungry.
2. We are late.
3. We are sad.
4. Do you like summer?
5. Do you like ice cream?
6. Do you like watermelons?
7. Close the door, please.
8. Close the book, please.
9. Close the window, please.

Ⓑ 1. 그녀는 정말 용감해!
2. 너의 이름은 뭐니?
3. 조용히 해주세요.

Chapter 2 명사와 관사

Unit 1 셀 수 있는 명사 문장 쓰기 노트 p.6

Ⓐ 1. I have two pencils.
2. She has three children.
3. Wolves have teeth.
4. I like strawberries.
5. He likes cats.
6. I like potatoes.
7. I need two dishes.
8. I need five fish.
9. I need ten books.

Ⓑ 1. 나는 두 개의 상자가 보여.
2. 내 발은 작아.
3. 그 소년은 세 개의 공을 가지고 있어.

Unit 2 셀 수 없는 명사 문장 쓰기 노트 p.7

Ⓐ 1. I have a piece of paper.
2. I have two bags of fruit.
3. I have two loaves of bread.
4. I drink a glass of juice.
5. I drink a glass of milk.
6. I drink a glass of water.
7. He is from Spain.
8. I am from Korea.
9. She is from Canada.

B 1. 이 사람은 다니엘이야.

2. 내 생일은 3월이야.

3. 나는 음악을 매우 좋아해.

Unit 3 부정관사 a/an   문장 쓰기 노트 p.8

A 1. It is a car.

2. It is an ant.

3. It is a piano.

4. I have an umbrella.

5. The chicken has an egg.

6. I have an old shirt.

7. I want to be an doctor.

8. I want to be an actor.

9. I want to be a teacher.

B 1. 거북이는 느려.

2. 그는 아이스크림을 사.

3. 문어는 다리가 여덟 개 있어.

Unit 4 정관사 the   문장 쓰기 노트 p.9

A 1. I play the cello.

2. I play the guitar.

3. I play the piano.

4. The earth is round.

5. The sky is high.

6. The sun is big.

7. I see the bear.

8. He sees the airplane.

9. I see the elephant.

B 1. 그 사과는 커.

2. 그 소금 좀 주세요.

3. 태양은 에너지를 만들어.

Chapter 03 대명사

Unit 1 주격 인칭대명사   문장 쓰기 노트 p.10

A 1. I play soccer.

2. They play basketball.

3. We play volleyball.

4. We are students.

5. They are my parents.

6. You are my friends.

7. She is funny.

8. It is new.

9. He is happy.

B 1. 그녀는 사람들을 도와.

2. 그것은 책이야.

3. 너는 내 여동생이야.

Unit 2 소유격 인칭대명사   문장 쓰기 노트 p.11

A 1. Her dress is yellow.

2. Their shirts are old.

3. His box is heavy.

4. It is your book.

5. He is my grandfather.

6. He is our teacher.

7. The cat plays with its toy.

8. They play with their blocks.

9. I play with my doll.

B 1. 그것은 내 우산이야.

2. 그녀의 미소는 아름다워.

3. 우리는 우리의 가방을 싸.

Unit 3 목적격 인칭대명사   문장 쓰기 노트 p.12

A 1. Mom loves me.

2. Dad loves us.

3. George loves her.

4. The doctor helps them.

5. The teacher helps me.

6. The firefighter helps us.

7. The students listen to her.

8. The children listen to me.

9. The animals listen to him.

B 1. 나는 그것을 원해.

2. 그것을 나에게 줘.

3. 그녀는 너를 알아.

Unit 4 소유대명사

Ⓐ 1. The roses are mine.
   2. The pencils are yours.
   3. The toys are his.
   4. I have yours.
   5. She has ours.
   6. We have yours.
   7. Theirs are on the sofa.
   8. Hers is on the desk.
   9. Yours is on the table.

Ⓑ 1. 그 그림들은 우리의 것이야.
   2. 그들의 것은 빨간색이야.
   3. 내 것은 어디 있어?

Unit 5 지시대명사　　문장 쓰기 노트 p.14

Ⓐ 1. This is a clock.
   2. That is a rabbit.
   3. This is a chair.
   4. These are apples.
   5. Those are grapes.
   6. Those are hats.
   7. This book is interesting.
   8. That police officer is brave.
   9. This train is fast.

Ⓑ 1. 이 학생들은 친절해.
   2. 저분들은 수미의 부모님이야.
   3. 저 꽃은 향이 좋아.

Unit 6 비인칭주어 it　　문장 쓰기 노트 p.15

Ⓐ 1. It is rainy.
   2. It is windy.
   3. It is snowy.
   4. It is spring.
   5. It is summer.
   6. It is winter.
   7. It is Monday.
   8. It is Friday.
   9. It is Sunday.

Ⓑ 1. 추워.
   2. 12월 25일이야.
   3. 세 시야.

Chapter 04 be동사

Unit 1 be동사 am, are, is　　문장 쓰기 노트 p.16

Ⓐ 1. I am a pianist.
   2. He is a nurse.
   3. She is a dentist.
   4. We are happy.
   5. You are smart.
   6. They are sleepy.
   7. Michael is in the classroom.
   8. My sisters are in Florida.
   9. Cars are in the parking lot.

Ⓑ 1. 당신은 아름다워요.
   2. 나는 비행기 조종사야.
   3. 그 펜은 책상 위에 있어.

Unit 2 be동사 긍정문과 부정문 문장 쓰기 노트 p.17

Ⓐ 1. He is a cashier.
   2. I am a lawyer.
   3. She is an artist.
   4. We are not old.
   5. They are not lazy.
   6. You are not excited.
   7. I am at the library.
   8. He is at the museum.
   9. They are at the zoo.

Ⓑ 1. 나는 아프지 않아.
   2. 우리는 춥지 않아.
   3. 그것은 내 주머니 안에 없어.

Unit 3 be동사 의문문　　문장 쓰기 노트 p.18

Ⓐ 1. Are you late?
   2. Are you okay?

3. Are you hungry?
4. Is he your grandfather?
5. Is she your friend?
6. Is he your brother?
7. Are they monkeys?
8. Are they bugs?
9. Are they Chinese?

Ⓑ 1. 네가 메리니?
2. 그들은 서울에 있니?
3. 그는 축구 선수니?

Chapter 05 일반동사

Unit 1 일반동사 현재형   문장 쓰기 노트 p.19

Ⓐ 1. They study English.
2. Harry studies math.
3. She studies science.
4. Jennifer goes to the cafe.
5. Tom goes to the library.
6. They go to the park.
7. My mom drinks coffee.
8. The children drink milk.
9. We drink water.

Ⓑ 1. 그는 런던에 살아.
2. 그들은 라디오를 들어.
3. 나는 영화를 봐.

Unit 2 일반동사 부정문   문장 쓰기 노트 p.20

Ⓐ 1. I don't like fishing.
2. You don't like cucumbers.
3. We don't like cheese.
4. He doesn't drive a car.
5. I don't drive a bus.
6. She doesn't drive a truck.
7. They don't eat vegetables.
8. He doesn't eat grapes.
9. I don't eat peanuts.

Ⓑ 1. 그들은 안경을 끼지 않아.

2. 그는 학교에 가지 않아.
3. 나는 야구를 하지 않아.

Unit 3 일반동사 의문문   문장 쓰기 노트 p.21

Ⓐ 1. Do you like carrots?
2. Does she like corn?
3. Do they like peaches?
4. Do you need crayons?
5. Do you need erasers?
6. Do we need chairs?
7. Do you remember the story?
8. Does he remember the movie?
9. Do you remember the book?

Ⓑ 1. 그것은 작동되니?
2. 너는 피아노를 치니?
3. 그는 목이 아프니?

Chapter 06 시제

Unit 1 현재진행형   문장 쓰기 노트 p.22

Ⓐ 1. You are riding a swing.
2. He is riding a bike.
3. She is riding a horse.
4. I'm not playing computer games.
5. They aren't playing basketball.
6. You aren't playing soccer.
7. Is Jane sleeping?
8. Is he playing?
9. Are you working?

Ⓑ 1. 우리는 저녁을 먹고 있어.
2. 너는 숙제를 하고 있니?
3. 눈이 오고 있지 않아.

Unit 2 be동사 과거형   문장 쓰기 노트 p.23

Ⓐ 1. He was happy.
2. They were sad.
3. It was heavy.

4. He wasn't a baseball player.

5. She wasn't a cook.

6. I wasn't a scientist.

7. Were you sick?

8. Was she hungry?

9. Were they thirsty?

Ⓑ 1. 그는 나의 선생님이었어.

2. 그들은 시끄럽지 않았어.

3. 그 고양이는 방 안에 있었니?

Unit 3 일반동사 과거형 문장 쓰기 노트 p.24

Ⓐ 1. He dropped the ball.

2. I dropped the cup.

3. You dropped the pen.

4. The boy ran to the house.

5. I ran to the store.

6. She ran to the school.

7. The children shared the snack.

8. They shared the cake.

9. We shared the food.

Ⓑ 1. 나는 나의 삼촌에게 편지를 썼어.

2. 사라는 사슴 한 마리를 보았어.

3. 그는 질문을 했어.

Unit 4 일반동사 과거형 부정문과 의문문 문장 쓰기 노트 p.25

Ⓐ 1. I didn't buy apples.

2. We didn't buy notebooks.

3. They didn't buy toys.

4. Did he clean his room?

5. Did she clean her car?

6. Did they clean their classroom?

7. Did you see stars?

8. Did they see giraffes?

9. Did you see zebras?

Ⓑ 1. 그는 동물원에 갔니?

2. 너는 눈사람을 만들었니?

3. 그 소녀는 머리를 빗지 않았어.

Unit 5 동사의 미래형 (will, be going to) 문장 쓰기 노트 p.26

Ⓐ 1. I will go to the hospital.

2. He will go to the library.

3. She will go to the supermarket.

4. He will not cry.

5. They will not run.

6. We will not swim.

7. Will you visit your teacher?

8. Will you visit your uncle?

9. Will you visit your grandparents?

Ⓑ 1. 나는 새 책을 살 거야.

2. 우리는 운동하지 않을 거야.

3. 그는 영화를 볼 거야.

Chapter 07 형용사와 부사

Unit 1 형용사의 의미와 쓰임 문장 쓰기 노트 p.27

Ⓐ 1. The teacher is kind.

2. The airplane is fast.

3. The train is long.

4. It is a red bicycle.

5. It is a blue backpack.

6. It is a yellow duck.

7. He has a beautiful daughter.

8. They have an old house.

9. She has a new watch.

Ⓑ 1. 그 개는 커.

2. 나는 장미 열 송이가 있어.

3. 상어들은 깊은 바다에 살아.

Unit 2 수량형용사 문장 쓰기 노트 p.28

Ⓐ 1. I have many books.

2. He has many friends.

3. I have many coins.

4. All children are lovely.

5. All tickets are expensive.

6. All students are excited.

7. I have some money.

8. She has some bread.

9. We have some time.

B 1. 나는 음식을 많이 먹지 않았어.

2. 모든 학생들은 책상이 있어.

3. 그는 어떠한 질문도 없었어.

Unit 3 **부사의 의미와 쓰임**   문장 쓰기 노트 p.29

A 1. Air is very important.

2. Sunlight is very warm.

3. Water is very helpful.

4. He runs fast.

5. She walks slowly.

6. They jump high.

7. She cried very sadly.

8. I smiled very happily.

9. He spoke very carefully.

B 1. 이것은 정말 맛있어.

2. 그는 정중하게 대답했어.

3. 나는 그 시험을 위해 열심히 공부했어.

Unit 4 **빈도부사**   문장 쓰기 노트 p.30

A 1. I always love you.

2. I always drink water.

3. I always draw pictures.

4. They often make gimbap.

5. She often makes pizza.

6. We often make salad.

7. I sometime play the piano.

8. He sometimes plays basketball.

9. They sometimes play tennis.

B 1. 그 상점은 보통 붐벼.

2. 그녀는 절대로 버거를 먹지 않아.

3. 보스턴에는 자주 눈이 와.

Chapter 08 비교급과 전치사

Unit 1 **비교급**   문장 쓰기 노트 p.31

A 1. He is taller than me.

2. She is smarter than him.

3. I am stronger than you.

4. They are more famous than us.

5. This is more delicious than that.

6. You are more beautiful than her.

7. I am happier than you.

8. Apples are bigger than cherries.

9. She is busier than me.

B 1. 오늘이 어제보다 더 좋아.

2. 그는 너보다 어려.

3. 그녀는 우리보다 지혜로워.

Unit 2 **최상급**   문장 쓰기 노트 p.32

A 1. I am the fastest in my class.

2. He is the youngest in my family.

3. She is the tallest in my class.

4. He is the most famous actor in the world.

5. It is the most delicious pie in the world.

6. She is the most beautiful woman in the world.

7. It is the highest mountain in Korea.

8. It is the largest elephant in America.

9. It is the longest road in China.

B 1. 그것은 하늘에서 가장 큰 별이야.

2. 그들은 그 도시에서 최고의 팀이야.

3. 축구는 한국에서 가장 인기있는 스포츠야.

Unit 3 **시간 전치사**   문장 쓰기 노트 p.33

A 1. I was born in 2002.

2. The baby was born in May.

3. He was born in 1920.

4. The test is on Monday.

5. The picnic is on Friday.

6. The meeting is on Wednesday.

7. I will go to the park after school.

8. He will meet Mia after Tuesday.

9. They will watch TV after 6 o'clock.

Ⓑ 1. 내 생일은 2월 14일이야.

2. 그 버스는 2시 30분에 와.

3. 나는 네 시 전에 돌아올 거야.

Unit 4 장소/방향 전치사   문장 쓰기 노트 p.34

Ⓐ 1. A cat is on the desk.

2. A cat is in the box.

3. A cat is under the chair.

4. A puppy is next to the ball.

5. A puppy is behind the tree.

6. A puppy is in front of the door.

7. I am from Seoul.

8. We are from France.

9. They are from Busan.

Ⓑ 1. 그들은 도서관에 갈 거야.

2. 그 책은 책가방 안에 있어.

3. 너의 안경은 탁자 위에 있어.

Unit 5 There is, There are   문장 쓰기 노트 p.35

Ⓐ 1. There is a pen on the book.

2. There is a candy in the drawer.

3. There is a boy next to the tree.

4. There are some flowers in the vase.

5. There are two books on the desk.

6. There are many oranges in the basket.

7. There aren't any bags under the table.

8. There aren't any notebooks on the table.

9. There aren't any toys under the table.

Ⓑ 1. 소파 위에 고양이가 있니?

2. 동물원에 곰들이 있니?

3. 냉장고 안에 우유가 없어.

Chapter 9 조동사

Unit 1 can   문장 쓰기 노트 p.36

Ⓐ 1. I can speak English.

2. He can speak Chinese.

3. She can speak French.

4. You can't fix the car.

5. We can't fix the computer.

6. They can't fix the roof.

7. Can you swim?

8. Can she cook?

9. Can he drive?

Ⓑ 1. 그는 이야기를 쓸 수 있어.

2. 나는 산을 탈 수 없어.

3. 제가 공원에 가도 되나요?

Unit 2 may   문장 쓰기 노트 p.37

Ⓐ 1. You may play with your toy.

2. She may play with her friends.

3. He may play with my dog.

4. You may not speak loud.

5. You may not come late.

6. You may not leave early.

7. May I use this chair?

8. May I use this pen?

9. May I use this door?

Ⓑ 1. 너는 물에서 놀아도 돼.

2. 너는 축구를 할 수 없어.

3. 제가 들어가도 되나요?

Unit 3 must, should   문장 쓰기 노트 p.38

Ⓐ 1. I must study.

2. You must hurry.

3. They must wait.

4. You must not run.

5. You must not eat.

6. He must not stop.

7. I should help her.

8. You should read more books.

9. He should drive slowly.

Ⓑ 1. 우리는 조용히 해야 해.

2. 당신은 여기에 주차할 수 없습니다.

3. 너는 집에 머물러야 해.

Chapter 10 동명사와 to부정사

Unit 1 동명사   문장 쓰기 노트 p.39

Ⓐ 1. Baking is her hobby.

2. Fishing is his hobby.

3. Dancing is my hobby.

4. I enjoy swimming.

5. He enjoys skating.

6. We enjoy cooking.

7. His job is delivering pizza.

8. My dream is making music.

9. My job is teaching children.

Ⓑ 1. 기타 치는 것은 재미있어.

2. 그는 한국어 말하는 것을 연습해.

3. 내 계획은 이모를 방문하는 거야.

Unit 2 to부정사   문장 쓰기 노트 p.40

Ⓐ 1. I like to learn.

2. She likes to swim.

3. He likes to sing.

4. I have a movie to watch.

5. We have a book to read.

6. They have a plan to play.

7. I am happy to meet you.

8. We are happy to win the game.

9. I am happy to pass the exam.

Ⓑ 1. 그의 꿈은 세계를 여행하는 거야.

2. 나는 마실 약간의 주스가 있어.

3. 그는 나를 보기 위해 왔어.

Chapter 11 접속사와 명령문

Unit 1 접속사   문장 쓰기 노트 p.41

Ⓐ 1. These are dogs and cats.

2. They are teachers and students.

3. We are happy and thankful.

4. He is old but funny.

5. They are tired but excited.

6. I am slow but steady.

7. He drank water because he was thirsty.

8. She was late because she missed the bus.

9. He was tired because he played hard.

Ⓑ 1. 비가 와서 나는 집에 있었어.

2. 쇠고기 먹을래, 아니면 치킨 먹을래?

3. 나는 열심히 공부해서 시험에 통과했어.

Unit 2 일반동사 명령문   문장 쓰기 노트 p.42

Ⓐ 1. Please open the door.

2. Please come early.

3. Please have a seat.

4. Do not feed the animals.

5. Do not touch the animals.

6. Do not hurt the animals.

7. Don't talk loud.

8. Don't take pictures.

9. Don't use plastic bags.

Ⓑ 1. 너의 방을 청소해주렴.

2. 너무 많이 먹지 마.

3. 네 숙제를 잊지 마.

Unit 3 be동사 명령문   문장 쓰기 노트 p.43

Ⓐ 1. Be brave.

2. Be quiet.

3. Be careful.

4. Don't be late.

5. Don't be sad.

6. Don't be afraid.

7. Be nice to your friends.

8. Be polite to people.
9. Be friendly to your brother.

Ⓑ 1. 화내지 마.
   2. 인내심을 가지세요.
   3. 미안해하지 마.

Chapter 12 의문사

Unit 1 what, which   문장 쓰기 노트 p.44

Ⓐ 1. What is your name?
   2. What is your address?
   3. What is your hobby?
   4. Which is her backpack?
   5. Which is his jacket?
   6. Which is my ball?
   7. What color do you like?
   8. What subject does he like?
   9. What animal does she like?

Ⓑ 1. 몇 시예요?
   2. 이 셔츠의 사이즈가 뭐예요?
   3. 너는 이것과 저것 중 어떤 게 더 좋아?

Unit 2 who, whose   문장 쓰기 노트 p.45

Ⓐ 1. Who was at the playground?
   2. Who was at the office?
   3. Who was at the classroom?
   4. Who is playing the violin?
   5. Who is playing the piano?
   6. Who is playing the guitar?
   7. Whose doll is it?
   8. Whose brother is he?
   9. Whose birthday is it?

Ⓑ 1. 누가 늦었니?
   2. 누가 사진을 찍고 있니?
   3. 그것은 누구의 애완동물이니?

Unit 3 when, where   문장 쓰기 노트 p.46

Ⓐ 1. When do you exercise?
   2. When does he study?
   3. When do you go to bed?
   4. Where is your friend?
   5. Where is his teacher?
   6. Where are her parents?
   7. Where do you live?
   8. Where do I sit?
   9. Where do you hurt?

Ⓑ 1. 너는 어디에서 태어났니?
   2. 너의 생일은 언제니?
   3. 너는 어디를 여행하고 싶니?

Unit 4 how, why   문장 쓰기 노트 p.47

Ⓐ 1. How old is she?
   2. How long is your hair?
   3. How far is the museum?
   4. How do you go to school?
   5. How do you go to work?
   6. How do you go to Dokdo?
   7. Why is he happy?
   8. Why are you tired?
   9. Why are they excited?

Ⓑ 1. 어떻게 지내?
   2. 너는 왜 울고 있니?
   3. 이 모자는 얼마예요?

Memo

Memo

Memo

한 권으로 끝내는 초등 영문법

문장 쓰기 노트

Happy House

한 권으로 끝내는 초등 영문법

초등

문장 쓰기 노트

Happy House

문장 쓰기 규칙

대문자 사용

- 영어 문장을 쓸 때 첫 글자는 항상 대문자로 시작해요.

  It is a cat. 그것은 고양이야.
  What is your name? 네 이름은 뭐니?

- 대명사 I 나 고유명사의 첫 글자는 문장의 어디에 오든지 항상 대문자로 써요.

  May I help you? 제가 도와드릴까요?
  They are Tim and Kate. 그들은 팀과 케이트야.

문장부호 사용

- 평서문의 끝에는 항상 마침표(.)를 찍어요.

  I like grapes. 나는 포도를 좋아해.

- 의문문의 끝에는 항상 물음표(?)를 찍어요.

  Do you have crayons? 너는 크레용을 갖고 있니?

- 감탄문의 끝에는 항상 느낌표(!)를 찍어요.

  How brave he is! 그는 정말 용감해!

띄어쓰기

단어와 단어 사이는 항상 띄어 써야 해요.
I^v love^v you. O   Iloveyou. X

정답은 본책 p.165에 있어요.

Ⓐ 우리말 문장을 읽고 영어로 알맞게 쓰세요.

1. 나는 내 **고양이**를 좋아해.
   (cat)
   → I like _____my_____ _____cat_____.

2. 나는 내 **강아지**를 좋아해.
   (puppy)
   → I like _____ _____.

3. 나는 내 **선생님**을 좋아해.
   (teacher)
   → _____

4. 그건 **노란색 버스**야.
   (yellow bus)
   → It is a _____ _____.

5. 그건 **갈색 말**이야.
   (brown horse)
   → It is _____ _____ _____.

6. 그건 **초록색 나무**야.
   (green tree)
   → _____

7. 그는 **축구공**을 가지고 있어.
   (soccer ball)
   → He has a _____ _____.

8. 그녀는 **컵**을 가지고 있어.
   (cup)
   → She has _____ _____.

9. 그는 **책**을 가지고 있어.
   (book)
   → _____

Ⓑ 영어 문장을 읽고 우리말 뜻을 쓰세요.

1. The stars are in the sky.
   → _____

2. They are students.
   → _____

3. I eat breakfast every day.
   → _____

3

정답은 본책 p.165에 있어요.

Ⓐ 우리말 문장을 읽고 영어로 알맞게 쓰세요.

1. 그는 **민호**야.
   (Minho)
   → He is ___Minho___.

2. 그는 **내 아빠**야.
   (dad)
   → He is ___my___ _____.

3. 그는 **내 친구**야.
   (friend)
   → _____

4. 나는 **야구와 농구**를 좋아해.
   (baseball, basketball)
   → I like _____ and _____.

5. 나는 **사과와 오렌지**를 좋아해.
   (apples, oranges)
   → I like _____ _____ _____.

6. 나는 **제니와 팀**을 좋아해.
   (Jenny, Tim)
   → _____

7. 꽃은 매우 **아름다워**.
   (beautiful)
   → Flowers are very _____.

8. 그 개는 매우 **귀여워**.
   (cute)
   → The dog is _____ _____.

9. 그 우유는 매우 **뜨거워**.
   (milk, hot)
   → _____

Ⓑ 영어 문장을 읽고 우리말 뜻을 쓰세요.

1. Frogs jump high.
   → _____

2. We sleep at night.
   → _____

3. She is tall.
   → _____

Ⓐ 우리말 문장을 읽고 영어로 알맞게 쓰세요.

1. 우리는 배가 고파.
   (hungry)
   → We are ___hungry___.

2. 우리는 늦었어.
   (late)
   → We _____ _____.

3. 우리는 슬퍼.
   (sad)
   → _____

4. 너는 **여름**을 좋아하니?
   (summer)
   → Do you like _____?

5. 너는 **아이스크림**을 좋아하니?
   (ice cream)
   → Do you _____ _____?

6. 너는 **수박**을 좋아하니?
   (watermelons)
   → _____

7. 문을 닫아주세요.
   (door)
   → Close the _____, please.

8. **책**을 덮어주세요.
   (book)
   → Close _____ _____, please.

9. **창문**을 닫아주세요.
   (window)
   → _____

Ⓑ 영어 문장을 읽고 우리말 뜻을 쓰세요.

1. How brave she is!
   → _____

2. What is your name?
   → _____

3. Please be quiet.
   → _____

5

정답은 본책 p.165에 있어요.

A 우리말 문장을 읽고 영어로 알맞게 쓰세요.

1. 나는 두 개의 **연필**이 있어.
   (pencils)
   → I have two ____pencils____.

2. 그녀는 세 명의 **아이들**이 있어.
   (children)
   → She has _____ _____.

3. 늑대들은 **이빨**을 가지고 있어.
   (wolves, teeth)
   → _____

4. 나는 **딸기**를 좋아해.
   (strawberries)
   → I like _____.

5. 그는 **고양이**를 좋아해.
   (cats)
   → He likes _____.

6. 나는 **감자**를 좋아해.
   (potatoes)
   → _____

7. 나는 **접시** 두 개가 필요해.
   (dishes)
   → I need two _____.

8. 나는 **물고기** 다섯 마리가 필요해.
   (fish)
   → I need _____ _____.

9. 나는 **책** 열 권이 필요해.
   (books)
   → _____

B 영어 문장을 읽고 우리말 뜻을 쓰세요.

1. I see two boxes.
   → _____

2. My feet are small.
   → _____

3. The boy has three balls.
   → _____

Chapter 02
Unit 2 셀 수 없는 명사

정답은 본책 p.165에 있어요.

Ⓐ 우리말 문장을 읽고 영어로 알맞게 쓰세요.

1. 나는 **종이** 한 장이 있어.
   (paper)
   → I have _____ a piece of _____ paper.

2. 나는 **과일** 두 봉지가 있어.
   (fruit)
   → I have _____ _____.

3. 나는 **빵** 두 덩어리가 있어.
   (bread)
   → _____

4. 나는 **주스** 한 잔을 마셔.
   (juice)
   → I drink _____ a glass of _____.

5. 나는 **우유** 한 잔을 마셔.
   (milk)
   → I drink _____ _____.

6. 나는 **물** 한 잔을 마셔.
   (water)
   → _____

7. 그는 **스페인** 출신이야.
   (Spain)
   → He is from _____.

8. 나는 **한국** 출신이야.
   (Korea)
   → I am _____ _____.

9. 그녀는 **캐나다** 출신이야.
   (Canada)
   → _____

Ⓑ 영어 문장을 읽고 우리말 뜻을 쓰세요.

1. This is Daniel.
   → _____

2. My birthday is in March.
   → _____

3. I love music.
   → _____

7

정답은 본책 p.166에 있어요.

Ⓐ 우리말 문장을 읽고 영어로 알맞게 쓰세요.

1. 그것은 **자동차**야.
   (car)
   → It is a ___car___.

2. 그것은 **개미**야.
   (ant)
   → It is _____ _____.

3. 그것은 **피아노**야.
   (piano)
   → _____

4. 나는 **우산**을 가지고 있어.
   (umbrella)
   → I have an _____.

5. 그 닭은 **달걀**을 가지고 있어.
   (egg)
   → The chicken has _____ _____.

6. 나는 **낡은 셔츠**를 가지고 있어.
   (old shirt)
   → _____

7. 나는 **의사**가 되고 싶어.
   (doctor)
   → I want to be a _____.

8. 나는 **배우**가 되고 싶어.
   (actor)
   → I want to be _____ _____.

9. 나는 **선생님**이 되고 싶어.
   (teacher)
   → _____

Ⓑ 영어 문장을 읽고 우리말 뜻을 쓰세요.

1. A turtle is slow.
   → _____

2. He buys an ice cream.
   → _____

3. An octopus has eight legs.
   → _____

정답은 본책 p.166에 있어요.

Ⓐ 우리말 문장을 읽고 영어로 알맞게 쓰세요.

1. 나는 **첼로**를 연주해.
   (cello)
   → I play the _____cello_____.

2. 나는 **기타**를 쳐.
   (guitar)
   → I play _____ _____.

3. 나는 **피아노**를 쳐.
   (piano)
   → _____

4. **지구**는 둥글어.
   (earth)
   → The _____ is round.

5. **하늘**은 높아.
   (sky)
   → _____ _____ is high.

6. **태양**은 커.
   (sun, big)
   → _____

7. 나는 그 **곰**이 보여.
   (bear)
   → I see the _____.

8. 그는 그 **비행기**가 보여.
   (airplane)
   → He sees _____ _____.

9. 나는 그 **코끼리**가 보여.
   (elephant)
   → _____

Ⓑ 영어 문장을 읽고 우리말 뜻을 쓰세요.

1. The apple is big.
   → _____

2. Please pass me the salt.
   → _____

3. The sun makes energy.
   → _____

9

Ⓐ 우리말 문장을 읽고 영어로 알맞게 쓰세요.

1. 나는 **축구**를 해.
(soccer)
→ I play __soccer__.

2. 그들은 **농구**를 해.
(basketball)
→ They _____ _____.

3. 우리는 **배구**를 해.
(volleyball)
→ _____.

4. 우리는 **학생**이야.
(students)
→ We are _____.

5. 그들은 **내 부모님**이야.
(parents)
→ They are ____my____ _____.

6. 너희들은 **내 친구**야.
(friends)
→ _____.

7. 그녀는 **재미있어**.
(funny)
→ She is _____.

8. 그것은 **새것**이야.
(new)
→ _____ is _____.

9. 그는 **행복해**.
(happy)
→ _____.

Ⓑ 영어 문장을 읽고 우리말 뜻을 쓰세요.

1. She helps people.
→ _____

2. It is a book.
→ _____

3. You are my sister.
→ _____

Ⓐ 우리말 문장을 읽고 영어로 알맞게 쓰세요.

1. 그녀의 **원피스**는 노란색이야.
   (dress)
   → ___Her___ ___dress___ is yellow.

2. 그들의 **셔츠**는 낡았어.
   (shirts)
   → _____ _____ are old.

3. 그의 **상자**는 무거워.
   (box, heavy)
   → _____

4. 그건 너의 **책**이야.
   (book)
   → It is _____ _____.

5. 그는 나의 **할아버지**야.
   (grandfather)
   → He is _____ _____.

6. 그는 우리의 **선생님**이야.
   (teacher)
   → _____

7. 그 고양이는 자기 **장난감**을 가지고 놀아.
   (toy)
   → The cat plays with _____ _____.

8. 그들은 그들의 **블럭**을 가지고 놀아.
   (blocks)
   → They play with _____ _____.

9. 나는 나의 **인형**을 가지고 놀아.
   (doll)
   → _____

Ⓑ 영어 문장을 읽고 우리말 뜻을 쓰세요.

1. It is my umbrella.
   → _____

2. Her smile is beautiful.
   → _____

3. We pack our bags.
   → _____

정답은 본책 p.166에 있어요.

Ⓐ 우리말 문장을 읽고 영어로 알맞게 쓰세요.

1. **엄마**는 나를 사랑해.
   (Mom)
   → _____Mom_____ loves me.

2. **아빠**는 우리를 사랑해.
   (Dad)
   → _____ loves _____.

3. **조지**는 그녀를 사랑해.
   (George)
   → _____

4. 그 **의사**는 그들을 돕는다.
   (doctor)
   → The _____ helps them.

5. 그 **선생님**은 나를 돕는다.
   (teacher)
   → The _____ helps _____.

6. 그 **소방관**은 우리를 돕는다.
   (firefighter)
   → _____

7. 그 **학생들**은 그녀의 말을 듣는다.
   (students)
   → The _____ listen to her.

8. 그 **아이들**은 나의 말을 듣는다.
   (children)
   → The _____ listen to _____.

9. 그 **동물들**은 그의 말을 듣는다.
   (animals)
   → _____

Ⓑ 영어 문장을 읽고 우리말 뜻을 쓰세요.

1. I want it.
   → _____

2. Give it to me.
   → _____

3. She knows you.
   → _____

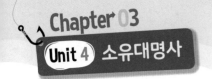

Chapter 03
Unit 4 소유대명사

정답은 본책 p.167에 있어요.

Ⓐ 우리말 문장을 읽고 영어로 알맞게 쓰세요.

1. 그 **장미**들은 내 것이야.
   (roses)
   → The ____roses___ are mine.

2. 그 **연필**들은 너의 것이야.
   (pencils)
   → The _____ are _____.

3. 그 **장난감**들은 그의 것이야.
   (toys)
   → _____

4. 내가 **너의 것**을 갖고 있어.
   (yours)
   → I have _____.

5. 그녀가 **우리의 것**을 갖고 있어.
   (ours)
   → _____ has _____.

6. 우리가 **너희들의 것**을 갖고 있어.
   (yours)
   → _____

7. **그들의 것**은 **소파** 위에 있어.
   (sofa)
   → _____ are on the sofa.

8. **그녀의 것**은 **책상** 위에 있어.
   (desk)
   → _____ is on the _____.

9. **너의 것**은 **탁자** 위에 있어.
   (table)
   → _____

Ⓑ 영어 문장을 읽고 우리말 뜻을 쓰세요.

1. The pictures are ours.
   → _____

2. Theirs is red.
   → _____

3. Where is mine?
   → _____

정답은 본책 p.167에 있어요.

Ⓐ 우리말 문장을 읽고 영어로 알맞게 쓰세요.

1. 이것은 **시계**야.
   (clock)
   → This is a _____clock_____.

2. 저것은 **토끼**야.
   (rabbit)
   → That is _____ _____.

3. 이것은 **의자**야.
   (chair)
   → _____

4. 이것들은 **사과들**이야.
   (apples)
   → These are _____.

5. 저것들은 **포도들**이야.
   (grapes)
   → Those are _____.

6. 저것들은 **모자들**이야.
   (hats)
   → _____

7. 이 **책**은 흥미로워요.
   (book)
   → This _____ is interesting.

8. 저 **경찰관**은 용감해요.
   (police officer)
   → That _____ _____ is brave.

9. 이 **기차**는 빨라요.
   (train, fast)
   → _____

Ⓑ 영어 문장을 읽고 우리말 뜻을 쓰세요.

1. These students are kind.
   → _____

2. Those are Sumi's parents.
   → _____

3. That flower smells nice.
   → _____

14

A 우리말 문장을 읽고 영어로 알맞게 쓰세요.

1. 비가 와.
   (rainy)
   → It is _____rainy_____.

2. 바람이 불어.
   (windy)
   → It is _____.

3. 눈이 와.
   (snowy)
   → _____

4. 봄이야.
   (spring)
   → _____

5. 여름이야.
   (summer)
   → _____

6. 겨울이야.
   (winter)
   → _____

7. 월요일이야.
   (Monday)
   → _____

8. 금요일이야.
   (Friday)
   → _____

9. 일요일이야.
   (Sunday)
   → _____

B 영어 문장을 읽고 우리말 뜻을 쓰세요.

1. It is cold.
   → _____

2. It is December 25.
   → _____

3. It is 3 o'clock.
   → _____

정답은 본책 p.167에 있어요.

Ⓐ 우리말 문장을 읽고 영어로 알맞게 쓰세요.

1. 나는 **피아니스트**야.
   (pianist)
   → I am a ___pianist___.

2. 그는 **간호사**야.
   (nurse)
   → He is _____ _____.

3. 그녀는 **치과 의사**야.
   (dentist)
   → _____

4. 우리는 **행복해**.
   (happy)
   → We are _____.

5. 너희들은 **똑똑해**.
   (smart)
   → You _____ _____.

6. 그들은 **졸려**.
   (sleepy)
   → _____

7. 마이클은 **교실**에 있어.
   (classroom)
   → Michael is in the _____.

8. 내 언니들은 **플로리다**에 있어.
   (Florida)
   → My sisters _____ in _____.

9. 자동차들은 **주차장**에 있어.
   (Cars, the parking lot)
   → _____

Ⓑ 영어 문장을 읽고 우리말 뜻을 쓰세요.

1. You are beautiful.
   → _____

2. I am a pilot.
   → _____

3. The pen is on the desk.
   → _____

Unit 2 be동사 긍정문과 부정문

정답은 본책 p.167에 있어요.

Ⓐ 우리말 문장을 읽고 영어로 알맞게 쓰세요.

1. 그는 **계산원**이야.
(cashier)
→ He is a ___cashier___.

2. 나는 **변호사**야.
(lawyer)
→ I am _____ _____.

3. 그녀는 **예술가**야.
(artist)
→ _____

4. 우리는 **늙지** 않았어.
(old)
→ We are not _____.

5. 그들은 **게으르지** 않아.
(lazy)
→ They are _____ _____.

6. 너희들은 **신나지** 않았어.
(excited)
→ _____

7. 나는 **도서관**에 있어.
(library)
→ I am at the _____.

8. 그는 **박물관**에 있어.
(museum)
→ He _____ at the _____.

9. 그들은 **동물원**에 있어.
(zoo)
→ _____

Ⓑ 영어 문장을 읽고 우리말 뜻을 쓰세요.

1. I'm not sick.
→ _____

2. We aren't cold.
→ _____

3. It is not in my pocket.
→ _____

정답은 본책 p.167에 있어요.

A 우리말 문장을 읽고 영어로 알맞게 쓰세요.

1. 너는 **늦었**니?
   (late)
   → Are you _____late_____?

2. 너는 **괜찮**니?
   (okay)
   → _____ you _____?

3. 너는 **배고프**니?
   (hungry)
   → _____

4. 그는 너의 **할아버지**니?
   (grandfather)
   → Is he your _____?

5. 그녀는 너의 **친구**니?
   (friend)
   → Is she _____ _____?

6. 그는 너의 **남동생**이니?
   (brother)
   → _____

7. 그것들은 **원숭이**들이니?
   (monkeys)
   → Are they _____?

8. 그것들은 **벌레**들이니?
   (bugs)
   → _____ they _____?

9. 그들은 **중국인**들이니?
   (Chinese)
   → _____

B 영어 문장을 읽고 우리말 뜻을 쓰세요.

1. Are you Mary?
   → _____

2. Are they in Seoul?
   → _____

3. Is he a soccer player?
   → _____

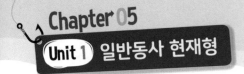

정답은 본책 p.168에 있어요.

A 우리말 문장을 읽고 영어로 알맞게 쓰세요.

1. 그들은 **영어**를 공부해.
   (English)
   → They study _____English_____.

2. 해리는 **수학**을 공부해.
   (math)
   → Harry _____ _____.

3. 그녀는 **과학**을 공부해.
   (science)
   → _____

4. 제니퍼는 그 **카페**에 가.
   (cafe)
   → Jennifer goes to the _____.

5. 톰은 그 **도서관**에 가.
   (library)
   → Tom _____ to the _____.

6. 그들은 그 **공원**에 가.
   (park)
   → _____

7. 우리 엄마는 **커피**를 마셔.
   (coffee)
   → My mom drinks _____.

8. 그 아이들은 **우유**를 마셔.
   (milk)
   → The children _____ _____.

9. 우리는 **물**을 마셔.
   (water)
   → _____

B 영어 문장을 읽고 우리말 뜻을 쓰세요.

1. He lives in London.
   → _____

2. They listen to the radio.
   → _____

3. I watch a movie.
   → _____

정답은 본책 p.168에 있어요.

Ⓐ 우리말 문장을 읽고 영어로 알맞게 쓰세요.

1. 나는 **낚시**를 좋아하지 않아.
   (fishing)
   → I don't like _____fishing_____.

2. 너는 **오이**를 좋아하지 않아.
   (cucumbers)
   → You don't like _____.

3. 우리는 **치즈**를 좋아하지 않아.
   (cheese)
   → _____

4. 그는 **차**를 운전하지 않아.
   (car)
   → He doesn't drive a _____.

5. 나는 **버스**를 운전하지 않아.
   (bus)
   → I _____ drive _____ _____.

6. 그녀는 **트럭**을 운전하지 않아.
   (truck)
   → _____

7. 그들은 **야채**를 먹지 않아.
   (vegetables)
   → They don't eat _____.

8. 그는 **포도**를 먹지 않아.
   (grapes)
   → He _____ eat _____.

9. 나는 **땅콩**을 먹지 않아.
   (peanuts)
   → _____

Ⓑ 영어 문장을 읽고 우리말 뜻을 쓰세요.

1. They don't wear glasses. → _____

2. He doesn't go to school. → _____

3. I don't play baseball. → _____

Ⓐ 우리말 문장을 읽고 영어로 알맞게 쓰세요.

1. 너는 **당근**을 좋아하니?
(carrots)
→ Do you like ____carrots____?

2. 그녀는 **옥수수**를 좋아하니?
(corn)
→ Does she _____ _____?

3. 그들은 **복숭아**를 좋아하니?
(peaches)
→ _____

4. 너는 **크레용**이 필요하니?
(crayons)
→ Do you need _____?

5. 너희들은 **지우개**가 필요하니?
(erasers)
→ Do you _____ _____?

6. 우리는 **의자**가 필요하니?
(chairs)
→ _____

7. 너는 그 **이야기**가 기억나니?
(story)
→ Do you remember the _____?

8. 그는 그 **영화**를 기억하니?
(movie)
→ _____ he remember _____ _____?

9. 너희들은 그 **책**이 기억나니?
(book)
→ _____

Ⓑ 영어 문장을 읽고 우리말 뜻을 쓰세요.

1. Does it work?
→ _____

2. Do you play the piano?
→ _____

3. Does he have a sore throat?
→ _____

21

Chapter 06
Unit 1 현재진행형

정답은 본책 p.168에 있어요.

A 우리말 문장을 읽고 영어로 알맞게 쓰세요.

1. 너는 **그네**를 타고 있어.
   (swing)
   → You are riding a ____swing____.

2. 그는 **자전거**를 타고 있어.
   (bike)
   → He is _____ _____ _____.

3. 그녀는 **말**을 타고 있어.
   (horse)
   → _____

4. 나는 **컴퓨터 게임**을 하고 있지 않아.
   (computer games)
   → I'm not playing _____ _____.

5. 그들은 **농구**를 하고 있지 않아.
   (basketball)
   → They aren't _____ _____.

6. 너는 **축구**를 하고 있지 않아.
   (soccer)
   → _____

7. 제인이 **자고** 있나요?
   (sleeping)
   → Is Jane _____?

8. 그는 **놀고** 있나요?
   (playing)
   → _____ he _____?

9. 당신은 **일하고** 있나요?
   (working)
   → _____

B 영어 문장을 읽고 우리말 뜻을 쓰세요.

1. We are having dinner.
   → _____

2. Are you doing your homework?
   → _____

3. It is not snowing.
   → _____

정답은 본책 p.168에 있어요.

A 우리말 문장을 읽고 영어로 알맞게 쓰세요.

1. 그는 **행복했어.**
   (happy)
   → He was ____happy____.

2. 그들은 **슬펐어.**
   (sad)
   → They _____ _____.

3. 그것은 **무거웠어.**
   (heavy)
   → _____

4. 그는 **야구 선수**가 아니었어.
   (baseball player)
   → He wasn't a _____ _____.

5. 그녀는 **요리사**가 아니었어.
   (cook)
   → She _____ _____ _____.

6. 나는 **과학자**가 아니었어.
   (scientist)
   → _____

7. 너는 **아팠니?**
   (sick)
   → Were you _____?

8. 그녀는 **배고팠니?**
   (hungry)
   → _____ she _____?

9. 그들은 **목이 말랐니?**
   (thirsty)
   → _____

B 영어 문장을 읽고 우리말 뜻을 쓰세요.

1. He was my teacher.
   → _____

2. They weren't noisy.
   → _____

3. Was the cat in the room?
   → _____

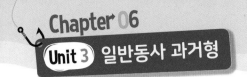

정답은 본책 p.169에 있어요.

Ⓐ 우리말 문장을 읽고 영어로 알맞게 쓰세요.

1. 그는 그 **공**을 떨어뜨렸어.
   (ball)
   → He dropped the _____.

2. 나는 그 **컵**을 떨어뜨렸어.
   (cup)
   → I dropped _____ _____.

3. 너는 그 **펜**을 떨어뜨렸어.
   (pen)
   → _____

4. 그 소년은 **집**으로 달려갔어.
   (house)
   → The boy ran to the _____.

5. 나는 그 **상점**으로 달려갔어.
   (store)
   → I ran to _____ _____.

6. 그녀는 **학교**로 달려갔어.
   (school)
   → _____

7. 그 아이들은 그 **간식**을 나눠먹었어.
   (snack)
   → The children shared the _____.

8. 그들은 그 **케이크**를 나눠먹었어.
   (cake)
   → They shared _____ _____.

9. 우리는 그 **음식**을 나눠먹었어.
   (food)
   → _____

Ⓑ 영어 문장을 읽고 우리말 뜻을 쓰세요.

1. I wrote a letter to my uncle. → _____

2. Sarah saw a deer. → _____

3. He asked a question. → _____

Ⓐ 우리말 문장을 읽고 영어로 알맞게 쓰세요.

1. 나는 **사과**를 사지 않았어.
(apples)
→ I didn't buy _____apples_____ .

2. 우리는 **공책**을 사지 않았어.
(notebooks)
→ We _____ buy _____ .

3. 그들은 **장난감**을 사지 않았어.
(toys)
→ _____

4. 그가 그의 **방**을 청소했니?
(room)
→ Did he clean his _____ ?

5. 그녀가 그녀의 **차**를 청소했니?
(car)
→ Did she _____ her _____ ?

6. 그들이 그들의 **교실**을 청소했니?
(classroom)
→ _____

7. 너는 **별**들을 보았니?
(stars)
→ Did you see _____ ?

8. 그들은 **기린**들을 보았니?
(giraffes)
→ _____ they see _____ ?

9. 너희들은 **얼룩말**들을 보았니?
(zebras)
→ _____

Ⓑ 영어 문장을 읽고 우리말 뜻을 쓰세요.

1. Did he go to the zoo?
→ _____

2. Did you make a snowman?
→ _____

3. The girl didn't brush her hair.
→ _____

Ⓐ 우리말 문장을 읽고 영어로 알맞게 쓰세요.

1. 나는 **병원**에 갈 거야.
(hospital)
→ I will go to the ___hospital___.

2. 그는 **도서관**에 갈 거야.
(library)
→ He will go to _____ _____.

3. 그녀는 **슈퍼마켓**에 갈 거야.
(supermarket)
→ _____

4. 그는 **울지** 않을 거야.
(cry)
→ He will not _____.

5. 그들은 **뛰지** 않을 거야.
(run)
→ They will _____ _____.

6. 우리는 **수영하지** 않을 거야.
(swim)
→ _____

7. 너는 네 **선생님**을 찾아뵐 거니?
(teacher)
→ Will you visit your _____?

8. 너는 네 **삼촌**을 찾아뵐 거니?
(uncle)
→ Will you _____ _____ _____?

9. 너는 네 **조부모님**을 찾아뵐 거니?
(grandparents)
→ _____

Ⓑ 영어 문장을 읽고 우리말 뜻을 쓰세요.

1. I'm going to buy a new book. → _____

2. We will not exercise. → _____

3. He's going to watch a movie. → _____

Ⓐ 우리말 문장을 읽고 영어로 알맞게 쓰세요.

1. 그 선생님은 친절해.
(teacher)
→ The _____teacher_____ is _____kind_____.

2. 그 비행기는 빨라.
(airplane)
→ _____ _____ is _____.

3. 그 기차는 길어.
(train)
→ _____

4. 그것은 빨간 자전거야.
(bicycle)
→ It is a red _____.

5. 그것은 파란 책가방이야.
(backpack)
→ It is _____.

6. 그것은 노란 오리야.
(duck)
→ _____

7. 그는 아름다운 딸이 있어.
(daughter)
→ He has a beautiful _____.

8. 그들은 오래된 집을 가지고 있어.
(house)
→ They have _____ _____ _____.

9. 그녀는 새 시계를 가지고 있어.
(watch)
→ _____

Ⓑ 영어 문장을 읽고 우리말 뜻을 쓰세요.

1. The dog is big.
→ _____

2. I have ten roses.
→ _____

3. Sharks live in the deep sea.
→ _____

Ⓐ 우리말 문장을 읽고 영어로 알맞게 쓰세요.

1. 나는 많은 **책들**을 가지고 있어.
   (books)
   → I have many ____books____.

2. 그는 많은 **친구들**을 가지고 있어.
   (friends)
   → He has _____ _____.

3. 나는 많은 **동전들**을 가지고 있어.
   (coins)
   → _____

4. 모든 아이들은 **사랑스러워**.
   (lovely)
   → All children are _____.

5. 모든 티켓들이 **비싸**.
   (expensive)
   → _____ tickets are _____.

6. 모든 학생들이 **신났어**.
   (excited)
   → _____

7. 나에게 **돈**이 조금 있어.
   (money)
   → I have some _____.

8. 그녀에게 **빵**이 조금 있어.
   (bread)
   → She has _____ _____.

9. 우리는 **시간**이 조금 있어.
   (time)
   → _____

Ⓑ 영어 문장을 읽고 우리말 뜻을 쓰세요.

1. I didn't eat much food.
   → _____

2. Every student has a desk.
   → _____

3. He didn't have any questions.
   → _____

정답은 본책 p.170에 있어요.

Ⓐ 우리말 문장을 읽고 영어로 알맞게 쓰세요.

1. 공기는 매우 **중요해요**.
   (important)
   → Air is very ___important___ .

2. 햇빛은 매우 **따뜻해요**.
   (warm)
   → Sunlight is _____ _____ .

3. 물은 매우 **유용해요**.
   (helpful)
   → _____

4. 그는 **빠르게** 뛰어.
   (fast)
   → He runs _____ .

5. 그녀는 **느리게** 걸어.
   (slowly)
   → She walks _____ .

6. 그들은 **높이** 점프해.
   (high)
   → _____

7. 그녀는 아주 **슬프게** 울었어.
   (sadly)
   → She cried very _____ .

8. 나는 아주 **행복하게** 미소지었어.
   (happily)
   → I smiled _____ _____ .

9. 그는 아주 **조심스럽게** 말했어.
   (spoke, carefully)
   → _____

Ⓑ 영어 문장을 읽고 우리말 뜻을 쓰세요.

1. This is really delicious.
   → _____

2. He answered politely.
   → _____

3. I studied hard for the test.
   → _____

Chapter 07
Unit 4 빈도부사

정답은 본책 p.170에 있어요.

Ⓐ 우리말 문장을 읽고 영어로 알맞게 쓰세요.

1. 나는 항상 너를 **사랑해**.
   (love)
   → I always ___love___ you.

2. 나는 항상 물을 **마셔**.
   (drink)
   → I always _____ _____.

3. 나는 항상 그림을 **그려**.
   (draw)
   → _____

4. 그들은 자주 **김밥**을 만들어.
   (gimbap)
   → They often make _____.

5. 그녀는 자주 **피자**를 만들어.
   (pizza)
   → She often _____ _____.

6. 우리는 자주 **샐러드**를 만들어.
   (salad)
   → _____

7. 나는 가끔 **피아노**를 쳐.
   (piano)
   → I sometimes play the _____.

8. 그는 가끔 **농구**를 해.
   (basketball)
   → He sometimes _____ _____.

9. 그들은 가끔 **테니스**를 쳐.
   (tennis)
   → _____

Ⓑ 영어 문장을 읽고 우리말 뜻을 쓰세요.

1. The store is usually busy.   → _____

2. She never eats burgers.   → _____

3. It often snows in Boston.   → _____

30

Ⓐ 우리말 문장을 읽고 영어로 알맞게 쓰세요.

1. 그는 나보다 더 키가 커.
   (taller)
   → He is ____taller____ than me.

2. 그녀는 그보다 더 똑똑해.
   (smarter)
   → She is _____ _____ _____.

3. 나는 너보다 더 힘이 세.
   (stronger)
   → _____

4. 그들은 우리보다 더 유명해.
   (more famous)
   → They are _____ _____ than us.

5. 이것이 저것보다 더 맛있어.
   (more delicious)
   → This is _____ _____ _____ that.

6. 네가 그녀보다 더 아름다워.
   (more beautiful)
   → _____

7. 나는 너보다 더 기뻐.
   (happier)
   → I am _____ _____ you.

8. 사과가 체리보다 더 커.
   (bigger)
   → Apples are _____ _____ cherries.

9. 그녀는 나보다 더 바빠.
   (busier)
   → _____

Ⓑ 영어 문장을 읽고 우리말 뜻을 쓰세요.

1. Today is better than yesterday. → _____

2. He is younger than you. → _____

3. She is wiser than us. → _____

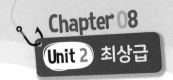

정답은 본책 p.170에 있어요.

Ⓐ 우리말 문장을 읽고 영어로 알맞게 쓰세요.

1. 나는 우리 반에서 **가장 빨라**.
   (fastest)
   → I am the ____fastest____ in my class.

2. 그는 우리 가족 중에서 **가장 어려**.
   (youngest)
   → He is _____ _____ in my family.

3. 그녀는 우리 반에서 **가장 키가 커**.
   (tallest)
   → _____

4. 그는 세상에서 **가장 유명한** 배우야.
   (most famous)
   → He is the _____ _____ actor in the world.

5. 그것은 세상에서 **가장 맛있는** 파이야.
   (most delicious)
   → It is _____ _____ _____
   pie in the world.

6. 그녀는 세상에서 **가장 아름다운**
   여성이야. (most beautiful)
   → _____

7. 그것은 한국에서 **가장 높은** 산이야.
   (highest)
   → It is the _____ mountain in Korea.

8. 그것은 미국에서 **가장 큰** 코끼리야.
   (largest)
   → It is _____ _____ _____
   in America.

9. 그것은 중국에서 **가장 긴** 도로야.
   (longest, road)
   → _____

Ⓑ 영어 문장을 읽고 우리말 뜻을 쓰세요.

1. It is the biggest star in the sky.
   → _____

2. They are the best team in the city.
   → _____

3. Soccer is the most popular sport
   in Korea.
   → _____

Chapter 08
Unit 3 시간 전치사

정답은 본책 p.170에 있어요.

Ⓐ 우리말 문장을 읽고 영어로 알맞게 쓰세요.

1. 나는 2002년에 태어났어.
   (2002)
   → I was born _____in_____ _____2002_____.

2. 그 아기는 5월에 태어났어.
   (May)
   → The baby was born _____ _____.

3. 그는 1920년에 태어났어.
   (1920)
   → _____

4. 그 시험은 **월요일**에 있어.
   (Monday)
   → The test is on _____.

5. 그 소풍은 **금요일**에 있어.
   (Friday)
   → The picnic is _____ _____.

6. 그 모임은 **수요일**에 있어.
   (Wednesday)
   → _____

7. 나는 **방과** 후에 공원에 갈 거야.
   (school)
   → I will go to the park after _____.

8. 그는 **화요일** 이후에 미아를 만날 거야.
   (Tuesday)
   → He will meet Mia _____ _____.

9. 그들은 **6시** 이후에 TV를 볼 거야.
   (watch TV, 6 o'clock)
   → _____

Ⓑ 영어 문장을 읽고 우리말 뜻을 쓰세요.

1. My birthday is on February 14th. → _____

2. The bus comes at 2:30. → _____

3. I'll come back before 4 o'clock. → _____

33

정답은 본책 p.171에 있어요.

Ⓐ 우리말 문장을 읽고 영어로 알맞게 쓰세요.

1. 고양이가 **책상** 위에 있어.
   (desk)
   → A cat is _____on_____ _____the_____ _____desk_____ .

2. 고양이가 **상자** 안에 있어.
   (box)
   → A cat is _____ _____ _____ .

3. 고양이가 **의자** 아래에 있어.
   (chair)
   → _____

4. 강아지가 **공** 옆에 있어.
   (ball)
   → A puppy is _____ _____ the ball.

5. 강아지가 **나무** 뒤에 있어.
   (tree)
   → A puppy is _____ .

6. 강아지가 **문** 앞에 있어.
   (door)
   → _____

7. 나는 **서울**에서 왔어.
   (Seoul)
   → I am from _____ .

8. 우리는 **프랑스**에서 왔어.
   (France)
   → We are _____ _____ .

9. 그들은 **부산**에서 왔어.
   (Busan)
   → _____

Ⓑ 영어 문장을 읽고 우리말 뜻을 쓰세요.

1. They will go to the library.
   → _____

2. The book is in the backpack.
   → _____

3. Your glasses are on the table.
   → _____

34

Chapter 08

Unit 5 There is, There are

정답은 본책 p.171에 있어요.

Ⓐ 우리말 문장을 읽고 영어로 알맞게 쓰세요.

1. 책 위에 **펜** 하나가 있어.
(pen)
→ There is a _____pen_____ on the book.

2. 서랍 안에 **사탕** 하나가 있어.
(candy)
→ There is _____ _____ in the drawer.

3. 나무 옆에 **소년** 한 명이 있어.
(boy)
→ _____

4. 꽃병 안에 **꽃**이 조금 있어.
(flowers)
→ There are some _____ in the vase.

5. 책상 위에 **책** 두 권이 있어.
(books)
→ There are _____ _____ on the desk.

6. 바구니 안에 **오렌지**가 많이 있어.
(oranges, basket)
→ _____

7. 탁자 밑에 어떤 **가방**도 없어.
(bags)
→ There aren't any _____ under the table.

8. 탁자 위에 어떤 **공책**도 없어.
(notebooks)
→ There _____ _____ _____ on the table.

9. 탁자 밑에 어떤 **장난감**도 없어.
(toys)
→ _____

Ⓑ 영어 문장을 읽고 우리말 뜻을 쓰세요.

1. Is there a cat on the sofa? → _____

2. Are there bears in the zoo? → _____

3. There isn't any milk in the fridge. → _____

35

정답은 본책 p.171에 있어요.

Ⓐ 우리말 문장을 읽고 영어로 알맞게 쓰세요.

1. 나는 **영어**를 말할 수 있어.
   (English)
   → I can speak ___English___.

2. 그는 **중국어**를 말할 수 있어.
   (Chinese)
   → He can _____ _____.

3. 그녀는 **프랑스어**를 말할 수 있어.
   (French)
   → _____

4. 너는 그 **차**를 고칠 수 없어.
   (car)
   → You can't fix the _____.

5. 우리는 그 **컴퓨터**를 고칠 수 없어.
   (computer)
   → We _____ fix _____ _____.

6. 그들은 그 **지붕**을 고칠 수 없어.
   (roof)
   → _____

7. 너는 **수영**할 수 있니?
   (swim)
   → Can you _____?

8. 그녀는 **요리**할 수 있니?
   (cook)
   → _____ she _____?

9. 그는 **운전**할 수 있니?
   (drive)
   → _____

Ⓑ 영어 문장을 읽고 우리말 뜻을 쓰세요.

1. He can write stories.
   → _____

2. I can't climb the mountain.
   → _____

3. Can I go to the park?
   → _____

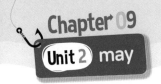

Ⓐ 우리말 문장을 읽고 영어로 알맞게 쓰세요.

1. 너는 네 **장난감**을 갖고 놀아도 돼. → You may play with your ____toy____.
(toy)

2. 그녀는 그녀의 **친구들**과 놀아도 돼. → She may play with _____ _____.
(friends)

3. 그는 나의 **개**와 놀아도 돼. → _____
(dog)

4. 당신은 **크게 이야기**할 수 없습니다. → You may not speak _____.
(loud)

5. 당신은 **늦게 올** 수 없습니다. → You may not _____ _____.
(late)

6. 당신은 **일찍 떠날** 수 없습니다. → _____
(leave, early)

7. 제가 이 **의자**를 사용해도 될까요? → May I use this _____?
(chair)

8. 제가 이 **펜**을 사용해도 될까요? → May I use _____ _____?
(pen)

9. 제가 이 **문**을 사용해도 될까요? → _____
(door)

Ⓑ 영어 문장을 읽고 우리말 뜻을 쓰세요.

1. You may play in the water. → _____

2. You may not play soccer. → _____

3. May I come in? → _____

정답은 본책 p.171에 있어요.

Ⓐ 우리말 문장을 읽고 영어로 알맞게 쓰세요.

1. 나는 **공부해야** 해.
(study)
→ I must ____study____.

2. 너는 **서둘러야** 해.
(hurry)
→ You _____ _____.

3. 그들은 **기다려야** 해.
(wait)
→ _____

4. 너희들은 **뛰어서는** 안돼.
(run)
→ You must not _____.

5. 너는 **먹어서는** 안돼.
(eat)
→ You must _____ _____.

6. 그는 **멈춰서는** 안돼.
(stop)
→ _____

7. 내가 그녀를 **도와야** 해.
(help)
→ I should _____ her.

8. 너는 더 많은 책을 **읽어야** 해.
(read)
→ You _____ _____ more books.

9. 그는 천천히 **운전해야** 해.
(drive, slowly)
→ _____

Ⓑ 영어 문장을 읽고 우리말 뜻을 쓰세요.

1. We must be quiet.
→ _____

2. You must not park here.
→ _____

3. You should stay home.
→ _____

정답은 본책 p.172에 있어요.

Ⓐ 우리말 문장을 읽고 영어로 알맞게 쓰세요.

1. **베이킹**은 그녀의 취미야. → _____Baking_____ is her hobby.
   (baking)

2. **낚시**는 그의 취미야. → _____ _____ his hobby.
   (fishing)

3. **춤추는 것**은 나의 취미야. → _____
   (dancing)

4. 나는 **수영하는** 것을 즐겨. → I enjoy _____.
   (swimming)

5. 그는 **스케이트 타는** 것을 즐겨. → He _____ _____.
   (skating)

6. 우리는 **요리하는** 것을 즐겨. → _____
   (cooking)

7. 그의 직업은 **피자를 배달하는** 거야. → His job is _____ _____.
   (delivering pizza)

8. 내 꿈은 **음악을 만드는** 거야. → My dream is _____ _____.
   (making music)

9. 내 직업은 **아이들을 가르치는** 거야. → _____
   (teaching children)

Ⓑ 영어 문장을 읽고 우리말 뜻을 쓰세요.

1. Playing the guitar is fun. → _____

2. He practices speaking Korean. → _____

3. My plan is visiting my aunt. → _____

정답은 본책 p.172에 있어요.

Ⓐ 우리말 문장을 읽고 영어로 알맞게 쓰세요.

1. 나는 **배우는** 것을 좋아해.
   (learn)
   → I like to ____learn____.

2. 그녀는 **수영하는** 것을 좋아해.
   (swim)
   → She likes _____ _____.

3. 그는 **노래하는** 것을 좋아해.
   (sing)
   → _____

4. 나는 **보려고** 하는 영화가 있어.
   (watch)
   → I have a movie to _____.

5. 우리는 **읽으려고** 하는 책이 있어.
   (read)
   → We have a book _____ _____.

6. 그들은 **놀려고** 하는 계획이 있어.
   (play)
   → _____

7. 나는 너를 **만나서** 기뻐.
   (meet)
   → I am happy to _____ you.

8. 우리는 그 게임에서 **이겨서** 기뻐.
   (win)
   → We are _____ _____ _____ the game.

9. 나는 시험에 **합격해서** 기뻐.
   (pass the exam)
   → _____

Ⓑ 영어 문장을 읽고 우리말 뜻을 쓰세요.

1. His dream is to travel the world. → _____

2. I have some juice to drink. → _____

3. He came to see me. → _____

Chapter 11
Unit 1 접속사

정답은 본책 p.172에 있어요.

A 우리말 문장을 읽고 영어로 알맞게 쓰세요.

1. 이것들은 강아지들과 고양이들이야. → These are _____dogs_____ and _____cats_____.
   (dogs, cats)

2. 그들은 선생님들과 학생들이야. → They are _____ _____ _____.
   (teachers, students)

3. 우리는 행복하고 감사해. → _____
   (happy, thankful)

4. 그는 나이가 많지만 재미있어. → He is _____ but _____.
   (old, funny)

5. 그들은 피곤하지만 신이 나. → They are _____ _____ _____.
   (tired, excited)

6. 나는 느리지만 꾸준히 해. → _____
   (slow, steady)

7. 그는 목이 말라서 물을 마셨어. → He drank water because he was _____.
   (thirsty)

8. 그녀는 버스를 놓쳐서 늦었어. → She was late _____.
   (missed the bus)

9. 그는 열심히 놀아서 피곤했어. → _____
   (played hard)

B 영어 문장을 읽고 우리말 뜻을 쓰세요.

1. It was raining, so I stayed at home. → _____

2. Do you want beef or chicken? → _____

3. I passed the test because I studied hard. → _____

41

ⓐ 우리말 문장을 읽고 영어로 알맞게 쓰세요.

1. 문을 **열어**주세요.
   (open)
   → Please _____ open _____ the _____ door _____.

2. 일찍 **와**주세요.
   (come)
   → _____ _____ early.

3. **앉아**주세요.
   (have a seat)
   → _____

4. 동물들을 **먹이지** 마세요.
   (feed)
   → Do not _____ the animals.

5. 동물들을 **만지지** 마세요.
   (touch)
   → Do not _____ _____ _____.

6. 동물들을 **다치게 하지** 마세요.
   (hurt)
   → _____

7. 크게 **말하지** 마세요.
   (talk)
   → Don't _____ loud.

8. **사진을 찍지** 마세요.
   (take pictures)
   → Don't _____ _____.

9. **비닐봉지를 사용하지** 마세요.
   (use plastic bags)
   → _____

ⓑ 영어 문장을 읽고 우리말 뜻을 쓰세요.

1. Clean your room, please.
   → _____

2. Don't eat too much.
   → _____

3. Don't forget your homework.
   → _____

정답은 본책 p.172에 있어요.

Ⓐ 우리말 문장을 읽고 영어로 알맞게 쓰세요.

1. 용감하게 해.
   (brave)
   → Be ___brave___.

2. 조용히 해.
   (quiet)
   → Be _____.

3. 조심해.
   (careful)
   → _____

4. 늦지 마.
   (late)
   → Don't be _____.

5. 슬퍼하지 마.
   (sad)
   → Don't _____ _____.

6. 두려워하지 마.
   (afraid)
   → _____

7. 너의 친구들에게 **친절히** 대해라.
   (nice)
   → Be _____ to your friends.

8. 사람들에게 **예의바르게** 행동해라.
   (polite)
   → Be _____ _____ people.

9. 너의 남동생에게 **친근하게** 대해라.
   (friendly)
   → _____

Ⓑ 영어 문장을 읽고 우리말 뜻을 쓰세요.

1. Don't be upset.
   → _____

2. Please be patient.
   → _____

3. Don't be sorry.
   → _____

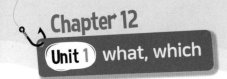

Chapter 12
Unit 1 what, which

정답은 본책 p.173에 있어요.

Ⓐ 우리말 문장을 읽고 영어로 알맞게 쓰세요.

1. 너의 **이름**이 뭐니?
   (name)
   → What is your _____name_____?

2. 너의 **주소**가 뭐니?
   (address)
   → What is _____ _____?

3. 너의 **취미**가 뭐니?
   (hobby)
   → _____

4. 어떤 것이 그녀의 **책가방**이니?
   (backpack)
   → Which is her _____?

5. 어떤 것이 그의 **재킷**이니?
   (jacket)
   → Which is _____ _____?

6. 어떤 것이 나의 **공**이니?
   (ball)
   → _____

7. 너는 무슨 **색깔**을 좋아하니?
   (color)
   → What _____ do you like?

8. 그는 무슨 **과목**을 좋아하니?
   (subject)
   → What _____ _____ _____ like?

9. 그녀는 무슨 **동물**을 좋아하니?
   (animal)
   → _____

Ⓑ 영어 문장을 읽고 우리말 뜻을 쓰세요.

1. What time is it?
   → _____

2. What size is this shirt?
   → _____

3. Which do you like better, this or that?
   → _____

44

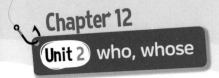

정답은 본책 p.173에 있어요.

A 우리말 문장을 읽고 영어로 알맞게 쓰세요.

1. 놀이터에 누가 있었니?
   (playground)
   → Who was at the __playground__ ?

2. 사무실에 누가 있었니?
   (office)
   → Who was _____ _____ _____?

3. 교실에 누가 있었니?
   (classroom)
   → _____

4. 누가 바이올린을 연주하고 있니?
   (violin)
   → Who is playing the _____?

5. 누가 피아노를 치고 있니?
   (piano)
   → Who is _____ _____ _____?

6. 누가 기타를 치고 있니?
   (guitar)
   → _____

7. 그것은 누구의 인형이니?
   (doll)
   → Whose _____ is it?

8. 그는 누구의 남동생이니?
   (brother)
   → Whose _____ _____ _____?

9. 누구의 생일이니?
   (birthday)
   → _____

B 영어 문장을 읽고 우리말 뜻을 쓰세요.

1. Who was late?
   → _____

2. Who is taking pictures?
   → _____

3. Whose pet is it?
   → _____

정답은 본책 p.173에 있어요.

Ⓐ 우리말 문장을 읽고 영어로 알맞게 쓰세요.

1. 너는 언제 **운동하니**?
(exercise)
→ When do you _____exercise_____?

2. 그는 언제 **공부하니**?
(study)
→ _____ does he _____?

3. 너는 언제 **잠자리에 드니**?
(go to bed)
→ _____

4. 네 **친구**는 어디 있니?
(friend)
→ Where is your _____?

5. 그의 **선생님**은 어디 계시니?
(teacher)
→ Where is _____ _____?

6. 그녀의 **부모님**은 어디 계시니?
(parents)
→ _____

7. 너 어디 **사니**?
(live)
→ Where do you _____?

8. 제가 어디에 **앉을까요**?
(sit)
→ _____ do I _____?

9. 당신은 어디를 **다치셨나요**?
(hurt)
→ _____

Ⓑ 영어 문장을 읽고 우리말 뜻을 쓰세요.

1. Where were you born?
→ _____

2. When is your birthday?
→ _____

3. Where do you want to travel? → _____

Chapter 12
Unit 4 how, why

정답은 본책 p.173에 있어요.

A 우리말 문장을 읽고 영어로 알맞게 쓰세요.

1. 그녀는 **몇 살**이니?
   (old)
   → How _____old_____ is she?

2. 너의 머리카락은 **얼마나 기니**?
   (long)
   → _____ _____ is your hair?

3. 그 박물관은 **얼마나 머니**?
   (far, museum)
   → _____

4. 너는 어떻게 **학교**에 가니?
   (school)
   → How do you go to _____?

5. 당신은 어떻게 **직장**에 가세요?
   (work)
   → How do you go _____ _____?

6. 너는 어떻게 **독도**에 가니?
   (Dokdo)
   → _____

7. 그는 왜 **기쁘니**?
   (happy)
   → Why is he _____?

8. 너는 왜 **지쳤니**?
   (tired)
   → _____ are you _____?

9. 그들은 왜 **신났니**?
   (excited)
   → _____

B 영어 문장을 읽고 우리말 뜻을 쓰세요.

1. How are you?
   → _____

2. Why are you crying?
   → _____

3. How much is this cap?
   → _____

47

Memo

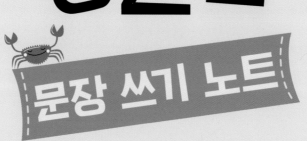

한 권으로 끝내는 초등 영문법

문장 쓰기 노트